GREATways to Teach and Learn™

Connect with Reading
Grade 2

Written by
Patricia Pedigo and Roger DeSanti

Edited and produced by
Patricia Pedigo

©2008 Plutarch Publications, Inc. PPI -1002

ISBN 978-1-934990-06-3

GREATways to Teach and Learn: Connect with Reading Grade 2
Published by
Plutarch Publications, Inc.
U.S.A.
Email (for customer service enquires): plutarch_inc@yahoo.com
Copyright© 2008 Plutarch Publications, Inc.

For Alyssa

Copyright © 2008, Plutarch Publications, Inc., Mandeville, Louisiana. All rights reserved. The purchase of this material entitles the buyer to reproduce worksheets and activities for classroom use only—not for commercial resale. Reproduction of these materials for an entire school or district is prohibited. No part of this book may be reproduced (except as noted above), stored in a retrieval system, or transmitted in any form or by any means (mechanically, electronically, recording, etc.) without the prior written consent of Plutarch Publications, Inc.

ISBN-13: 978-1-934990-06-3
ISBN-10: 1-934990-06-X

Connect With Reading Grade 2

How to Use This Book	1
Quick Cues Vocabulary	2
Quick Cues Vocabulary	3
Score Computation Chart	4
Standards Competency Chart	5

Vocabulary

Word Identification	6
Word Identification	7
Word Identification	8
Synonyms	9
Synonyms	10
Synonyms	11
Antonyms	12
Antonyms	13
Antonyms	14
Spelling	15
Spelling	16
Spelling	17

Decoding Skills

Blends	18
Blends	19
Blends	20
Blends	21
Vowels	22
Vowels	23
Vowels	24
Vowels	25
Context Clues	26
Context Clues	27
Context Clues	28
Context Clues	29

Concept Building

Sequence of Events	30
Sequence of Events	31
Sequence of Events	32
Fact/Opinion	33
Fact/Opinion	34
Fact/Opinion	35
Compare/Contrast	36
Compare/Contrast	37
Compare/Contrast	38
Story Elements	39
Story Elements	40
Story Elements	41
Genre	42

Comprehension *Narrative Stories*

Juan's Bike Ride	43
Roxie the Dog	44
Fluffy the Bunny	45
James' Hobby	46
Tamika and the Dolphin	47
Three Mice	48
Padma's Piano	49
Peter and the Dentist	50
Maria and Friends	51

Comprehension *Expository Stories*

Living or Nonliving?	52
Plants	53
Animals	54
Mammals	55
Birds	56
Fish	57
Reptiles	58
Amphibians	59
Insects	60

Comprehension

Poetry	61
Poetry	62
Poetry	63
Letters	64
Letters	65
Letters	66
Riddles	67
Riddles	68
Riddles	69

Answer Keys

Pages 6 - 9	70	Pages 38 - 41	78
Pages 10 - 13	71	Pages 42 - 45	79
Pages 14 - 17	72	Pages 46 - 49	80
Pages 18 - 21	73	Pages 50 - 53	81
Pages 22 - 25	74	Pages 54 - 57	82
Pages 26 - 29	75	Pages 58 - 61	83
Pages 30 - 33	76	Pages 62 - 65	84
Pages 34 - 37	77	Pages 66 - 69	85

©2008 Plutarch Publications, Inc. PPI -1002

About the series ...

The GREATways to Teach and Learn™ series are books intended to supplement curriculum and textbooks. Over sixty pages of activities presented in each GREATways to Teach and Learn™ book engage the learner in active practice of basic skills required at the appropriate grade level. Activities are designed with various learning styles in mind to include every child in the learning process.

Each book contains two pages of *Quick Cues*, a handy list of important vocabulary, rules, or examples of standards covered in that GREATways to Teach and Learn™ book. The page "How to Use This Book" provides suggestions and ideas for using *Quick Cues* for additional instruction or practice.

GREATways to Teach and Learn™ books are designed to comply with State Curriculum Standards. Although the level at which specific topics are mandated may vary from State to State, many State Curriculum Standards agree on the grade level at which most skills are introduced. The GREATways to Teach and Learn™ series focuses on those standards that are commonly introduced at each grade level. The Score Computation Chart (page 4) and the Standards Competency Chart (page 5) provide a viable means to assess the level at which a child is able to complete each standard presented.

The goal of this series is to provide grade appropriate standards, practice, and application in a straight-forward, easy to understand manner. Appropriate materials and presentation produce comprehension. Practice produces proficiency. Application produces students able to interact with the real world.

About the authors and editor .....

Patricia Pedigo, M.Ed. in elementary education, also earned the Reading Specialist endorsement. She has more than 20 years experience in elementary and junior high classrooms and a passion for working with "learning different" children. Patricia has authored and/or edited 50 instructional books that are used in classrooms across North America.

Roger DeSanti Sr., Ed.D. in Reading and Special Education, is a Professor of Education whose area of expertise is literacy and the learning process. He has over 30 years of classroom experience working with and educating children and their teachers. Roger has over 100 publications, including instructional books that are used in classrooms across North America.

How to use this book ...
GREATways: Instruction books offer several features designed to enhance the learning process and assist the teacher in assessing the learner's progress. On the next few pages you will find Quick Cues, a Score Computation Chart, a Standards Competency Chart, and recommendations based on the competency level of the learner.

QUICK CUES: This book includes two pages of *Quick Cues* which are important facts at your fingertips. The Quick Cues found on pages two and three of this book lists 160 words that should be part of the basic reading vocabulary of second grade learners. Ways to use these pages are as varied as the number of readers, but here are a few suggestions to get started:
- Have the learner scan a newspaper or magazine and try to find words from the *Quick Cues* list.
- Create a "Book of Words" where the learner places a word from the list on each page and adds an illustration
- Ask the learner to select ten of the words and use them in a story
- List each word on an index card and use them as flashcards. The learner can keep the words that are correctly identified.
- Create a "Word Bank" box where the flashcards can be kept. Have the learner use these words to create sentences or short stories.

SCORE COMPUTATION CHART: This assessment tool can be found on page four of this book. After the learner completes an activity in this book, record the number of correct items on the score computation chart. When all pages for a listed standard have been completed, tally the number of correct answers and record it in the column on the far right (under the total of correct answers possible). Transfer the learner's totals to the chart on page five to find the level of competency.

STANDARDS COMPETENCY CHART: Use the total number correct scores from page four to identify the level at which the learner comprehends/applies the standard. The range of scores within each level (Mastery, Instructional, Basic, and Limited) are approximate indicators of how well the learner understands and can apply each standard. The degree of competency at that level will vary with the score. For example, a score of 76 in Word Recognition indicates Mastery, but is close to Instructional and the learner could benefit from more practice with that standard. Recommendations based on the competency level are offered at the bottom of the page.

Quick Cues
Second Grade Word List

above	beyond	clock	excited
afraid	blanket	cloudy	extra
after	boat	cool	factory
afternoon	bottom	dash	favorite
alike	bread	difficult	feelings
angry	breakfast	dinner	fence
anybody	breeze	dirt	few
apart	bridge	downstairs	final
artist	bright	dragon	finger
asleep	brush	dress	finish
aunt	bush	dry	float
author	calendar	dust	forgot
balloon	careful	early	Friday
basement	carrot	east	frighten
beach	center	easy	garbage
bedroom	change	elevator	hour
before	cheese	empty	huge
behind	chicken	enter	indoor
below	child	evening	invite
bench	claws	everybody	kitchen

Quick Cues

Second Grade Word List

knee	ocean	sack	thin
leaf	once	sandwich	Thursday
leap	pail	Saturday	tight
learn	paper	scary	title
living	paste	sell	toothbrush
lonely	penny	shoes	towel
middle	piano	shoulder	trail
milk	picnic	sidewalk	Tuesday
minute	point	slide	twig
Monday	pond	softer	ugly
monster	poor	south	weather
month	popcorn	storm	Wednesday
morning	present	straight	week
mud	pretend	Sunday	west
music	quiet	sunny	whisper
nest	repair	swing	windy
newspaper	river	taste	woman
nobody	roof	teeth	wrote
nonliving	rough	terrible	yard
north	rush	their	year

Score Computation Chart

Connect with Reading

Grade 2

Word Recognition											Score
Page number	6	7	8	15	16	17					
# possible	16	16	16	12	12	12					84
# correct											
Synonym/Antonym											
Page number	9	10	11	12	13	14					
# possible	12	12	12	12	12	12					72
# correct											
Vowels/Blends											
Page number	18	19	20	21	22	23	24	25			
# possible	10	10	10	10	12	12	12	12			88
# correct											
Context Clues											
Page number	26	27	28	29							
# possible	10	10	10	10							40
# correct											
Sequence											
Page number	30	31	32								
# possible	36	32	5								73
# correct											
Fact or Opinion											
Page number	33	34	35								
# possible	22	22	22								66
# correct											
Compare/Contrast											
Page number	36	37	38								
# possible	15	15	15								45
# correct											
Elements/Genre											
Page number	39	40	41	42							
# possible	15	15	10	8							48
# correct											
Narrative Story											
Page number	43	44	45	46	47	48	49	50	51		
# possible	8	8	8	8	8	8	8	8	8		72
# correct											
Expository Story											
Page number	52	53	54	55	56	57	58	59	60		
# possible	20	20	20	20	20	20	20	20	20		180
# correct											
Functional Context											
Page number	61	62	63	64	65	66	67	68	69		
# possible	11	11	11	6	6	6	5	5	5		66
# correct											

©2008 Plutarch Publications, Inc. PPI -1002

Standards Competency Chart

Step 1: After the learner completes each page, record the number correct on the Score Computation Chart (page 4). Calculate the total number correct for each standard.

Step 2: Find the learner's score for each standard in the boxes of that row. Mark the box with an X (or the learner's score) to identify the level of competency for that standard. For example, a score of 56 for the standard of Narrative Passage places the child on the "Instructional" level and a score of 66 would indicate the "Mastery" level.

Step 3: Follow the recommendation guidelines at the bottom of this page.

Standard	Mastery	Instructional	Basic	Limited
Word Recognition	84 - 76	75 - 63	62 - 50	49 or below
Synonym/Antonym	72 - 65	64 - 54	53 - 43	42 or below
Vowels/Blends	88 - 79	78 - 66	65 - 53	52 or below
Context Clues	40 - 36	35 - 30	29 - 24	23 or below
Sequence	73 - 66	65 - 55	54 - 44	43 or below
Fact or Opinion	66 - 59	58 - 50	49 - 40	39 or below
Compare/Contrast	45 - 40	39 - 34	33 - 27	26 or below
Elements/Genre	48 - 43	42 - 36	35 - 29	28 or below
Narrative Passage	72 - 65	64 - 54	53 - 43	42 or below
Expository Passage	180 - 162	161 - 135	134 - 108	107 or below
Functional Passage	66 - 59	58 - 50	49 - 40	39 or below

Recommendation Guidelines

Mastery: The learner is capable of using this standard independently. Move on to the next higher grade level.

Instructional: The learner has a working understanding of the standard, but needs some guided practice on this grade level.

Basic: The learner has minimal grasp of the standard and needs direct instruction and guided practice to apply the concept fully. The learner could benefit from moving one grade level lower for review and extra practice before approaching the standard at this level once again.

Limited: The learner has a limited understanding of the standard and should be moved to the next lower grade level for instruction and practice.

©2008 Plutarch Publications, Inc. PPI -1002

Name _____   Standard: Word Identification

Look at each picture. Circle the word in each row that describes the picture. There are four words for each picture.

1. rainbow   river   rice
2. boat   build   bowl
3. shirt   sunny   stood
4. bench   bottle   bush

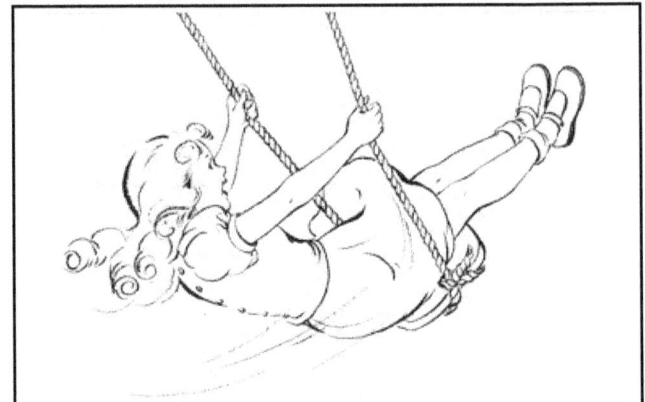

1. snap   speak   swing
2. chase   child   cheese
3. shoes   soft   suit
4. doorway   desk   dress

1. sandwich   state   spell
2. round   race   rode
3. throw   taste   teach
4. belt   bend   bread

1. answer   apart   airplane
2. cloudy   castle   chin
3. feather   fishing fly
4. wife   wing   worm

©2008 Plutarch Publications, Inc. PPI -1002

Name _____   Standard: Word Identification

Look at each picture. Circle the word in each row that describes the picture. There are four words for each picture.

1. arrow   asleep   artist
2. plate   phone   painting
3. brush   bush   burn
4. pack   picture   pillow

1. bedroom   barn   basement
2. leaf   lamp   lemon
3. dresser   deer   drop
4. whistle   wheel   windows

1. bank   baseball   bench
2. moon   map   mitt
3. soup   spend   slide
4. dollar   dust   drum

1. cattle   calendar   crab
2. mud   month   mile
3. yard   yet   year
4. point   pour   potato

©2008 Plutarch Publications, Inc. PPI-1002

Name _____   Standard: Word Identification

Look at each picture. Circle the word in each row that describes the picture. There are four words for each picture.

1. picnic   puppy   puzzle
2. basket   balloon   board
3. band   bunny   blanket
4. camera   circus   clap

1. donkey   dragon   deep
2. candle   coin   claws
3. tent   teeth   tickle
4. scary   spoon   skate

1. umbrella untie   uncle
2. string   storm   shut
3. wagon   wink   windy
4. wolf   weather   write

1. bell   bridge   bath
2. tape   towel   third
3. trail   twig   tub
4. soap   soil   sink

©2008 Plutarch Publications, Inc. PPI-1002   8

Name _____   Standard: Synonyms

SYNONYMS are words that have almost the **same meaning**. Circle the word or phrase that is a synonym for the underlined word in each sentence.

---

1. The shelf is <u>above</u> my head.

    beside   over

    under

2. I am <u>afraid</u> of spiders!

    angry   scared

    warm

3. Jan wants to go <u>also</u>.

    later   now

    too

4. Please do not be <u>angry</u> at me.

    mad   often

    silly

5. Your lips are just <u>below</u> your nose.

    behind   beyond

    under

6. It is a very <u>bright</u> day and I need my sunglasses!

    pretty   sunny

    windy

7. Please take off your <u>cap</u> when you come indoors.

    hat   mittens

    scarf

8. She put the flowers in the <u>center</u> of the table.

    back   middle

    side

9. Mom pours coffee into a <u>mug</u>.

    cup   glass

    plate

10. I will <u>dash</u> back to the house and get your jacket.

    call   jump

    run

11. We planted flower seeds in the <u>dirt</u>.

    bedroom   soil

    weeds

12. We will <u>enter</u> the house through the back door.

    go in   go out

    go to

©2008 Plutarch Publications, Inc. PPI -1002

Name _____   Standard: Synonyms

SYNONYMS are words that have almost the **same meaning**. Circle the word or phrase that is a synonym for the underlined word in each sentence.

1. Dad put <u>extra</u> cookies in my lunch. **any** **more** **some**	2. Judy was the <u>final</u> person in line. **first** **last** **only**
3. Put the paint away when you <u>finish</u>. **begin** **draw** **end**	4. That big dog <u>frightens</u> me! **fights** **growls** **scares**
5. Be sure to throw away your <u>garbage</u>. **plate** **trash** **trunk**	6. That was a <u>difficult</u> test! **easy** **hard** **jolly**
7. Many birds build nests in that <u>huge</u> tree. **big** **little** **tiny**	8. That <u>lady</u> is my neighbor. **girl** **lonely** **woman**
9. Can you <u>leap</u> over the fence? **gallop** **jump** **walk**	10. I went to the ocean <u>once</u> and saw a shark! **fish** **often** **one time**
11. Put the water in this <u>pail</u>. **bucket** **glass** **hole**	12. We can use <u>paste</u> to fix the tear in that paper. **butter** **glue** **wax**

©2008 Plutarch Publications, Inc. PPI -1002

Name _____

Standard: Synonyms

SYNONYMS are words that have almost the **same meaning**. Circle the word or phrase that is a synonym for the underlined word in each sentence.

1. The gum costs one <u>penny</u>.
 	
    cent   **dime**
 	
        dollar
	2. Sue got three <u>presents</u> for her birthday.
	
	    boxes **gifts**
	
	        stripes

3. Joe did his work <u>quickly</u>!
 	
    fast   **slow**
 	
        well
	4. The man had to <u>repair</u> the flat tire on his car.
	
	    bend **fix**
	
	        slide

5. Do not be in a <u>rush</u> to grow up!
 	
    busy   **drop**
 	
        hurry
	6. We put the groceries in a brown paper <u>sack</u>.
	
	    bag **truck**
	
	        wagon

7. Please <u>shut</u> the door to keep the rain out.
 	
    catch   **close**
 	
        slam
	8. Mrs. Jones ate too much and now she feels <u>sick</u>.
	
	    good **ill**
	
	        tired

9. We need more <u>space</u> to hang this big mirror.
 	
    clay   **nails**
 	
        room
	10. Will you <u>toss</u> that ball to me?
	
	    loose **roll**
	
	        throw

11. This <u>trail</u> goes right through the forrest.
 	
    path   **tree**
 	
        travel
	12. The bird used <u>twigs</u> to build a nest.
	
	    feathers **newspapers**
	
	        sticks

Name _____   Standard: Antonyms

ANTONYMS are words that have **opposite meanings**. Circle the word or phrase that is an antonym for the underlined word in each sentence.

1. Put this picture <u>above</u> the other on the wall. **below** **over** **next to**	2. Josh was <u>behind</u> you in line. **ahead of** **after** **next to**
3. Those sisters are <u>alike</u> in many ways. **almost** **different** **the same**	4. Jen was <u>angry</u> that she missed the party. **happy** **mad** **upset**
5. Those children are hard to keep <u>apart</u>. **away** **awake** **together**	6. The baby is <u>asleep</u> now. **awake** **eating** **napping**
7. Do your work <u>before</u> dinner. **after** **beside** **with**	8. Tape the <u>bottom</u> of the box. **below** **side** **top**
9. Would you like to <u>sell</u> those pencils? **buy** **take** **use**	10. The weather seems a little <u>cool</u> today. **cold** **snowy** **warm**
11. My bedroom is <u>downstairs</u>. **clean** **indoors** **upstairs**	12. The dishes are not <u>dry</u> yet. **done** **wet** **wild**

©2008 Plutarch Publications, Inc. PPI-1002

Name _____

Standard: Antonyms

ANTONYMS are words that have **opposite meanings**. Circle the word or phrase that is an antonym for the underlined word in each sentence.

1. Daddy came home <u>early</u> from work. **before**　　**late** **whenever**	2. It is <u>easy</u> to draw a flower. **fast**　　**fun** **hard**
3. The bucket is <u>empty</u>. **full**　　**lonely** **warm**	4. <u>Everybody</u> loved the school play! **All of us**　　**Nobody** **They**
5. Peter drew a <u>thin</u> line across the board. **bare**　　**careful** **wide**	6. There are <u>few</u> people who want to help. **busy**　　**less** **many**
7. I have the <u>final</u> piece of the puzzle! **first**　　**last** **shape**	8. It is time to <u>finish</u> your lunch. **own**　　**start** **stop**
9. I <u>forgot</u> where I put my book. **almost**　　**belong** **remembered**	10. Judy <u>loves</u> to watch scary movies. **favorite**　　**hates** **likes**
11. Kyle's mother made a <u>huge</u> pie for us to share. **big**　　**large** **tiny**	12. Be <u>quiet</u>. The baby is sleeping. **careful**　　**loud** **proud**

©2008 Plutarch Publications, Inc. PPI -1002

Name _____   Standard: Antonyms

ANTONYMS are words that have **opposite meanings**. Circle the word or phrase that is an antonym for the underlined word in each sentence.

---

1. We must play <u>indoors</u> today.

    inside   outside

    together

2. That <u>poor</u> family lives in the old house at the end of the street.

    nice   office

    rich

3. Father will <u>repair</u> the flat tire on my bike.

    break   fix

    sell

4. Your hand feels <u>rough</u> and dry.

    hard   sharp

    smooth

5. Please <u>shut</u> the door for me.

    close   find

    open

6. My pillow is <u>softer</u> than my blanket.

    better   harder

    nicer

7. The map shows that we need to go <u>south</u> on Elm Street.

    east   home

    north

8. Darla has <u>straight</u> hair.

    curly   fine

    thin

9. The weather is <u>terrible</u> today!

    awful   bad

    wonderful

10. My shoes are too <u>tight</u> and don't fit well.

    fresh   loose

    old

11. That <u>ugly</u> dog does great tricks!

    mean   pretty

    young

12. We must <u>whisper</u> in class.

    talk   whistle

    yell

©2008 Plutarch Publications, Inc. PPI-1002

Name _____   Standard: Spelling

One word in each group below is not spelled correctly. Put an **X** in the box next to the word that is <u>NOT</u> correct.

☐ yell ☐ frighten ☐ scary ☐ afrad	☐ backyard ☐ fense ☐ swing ☐ play	☐ twig ☐ stik ☐ tree ☐ forest
☐ bird ☐ robin ☐ nesst ☐ flew	☐ Monday ☐ Tuesday ☐ Wedesday ☐ Thursday	☐ nine ☐ sevn ☐ three ☐ six
☐ yaer ☐ month ☐ day ☐ week	☐ spring ☐ sumer ☐ fall ☐ winter	☐ sangwich ☐ milk ☐ lunch ☐ cookie
☐ wolf ☐ growl ☐ teth ☐ pack	☐ musick ☐ band ☐ piano ☐ lesson	☐ happy ☐ hope ☐ felt ☐ carefull

©2008 Plutarch Publications, Inc. PPI -1002

Name _____   Standard: Spelling

One word in each group below is not spelled correctly. Put an **X** in the box next to the word that is <u>NOT</u> correct.

☐ the ☐ there ☐ thier ☐ they're	☐ monster ☐ ugly ☐ screem ☐ scare	☐ beddroom ☐ lamp ☐ blanket ☐ quilt
☐ evening ☐ moonlight ☐ wind ☐ breze	☐ swing ☐ brige ☐ park ☐ pond	☐ boot ☐ mudd ☐ rain ☐ storm
☐ family ☐ dress ☐ aunt ☐ wooman	☐ donkie ☐ barn ☐ quack ☐ mice	☐ horse ☐ babby ☐ raccoon ☐ worm
☐ nobbody ☐ everybody ☐ anybody ☐ anyone	☐ basement ☐ roof ☐ hous ☐ yard	☐ befor ☐ after ☐ soon ☐ never

©2008 Plutarch Publications, Inc. PPI -1002

Name _____   Standard: Spelling

One word in each group below is not spelled correctly. Put an **X** in the box next to the word that is NOT correct.

☐ beach	☐ mountain	☐ write
☐ sand	☐ clim	☐ spell
☐ shor	☐ bush	☐ count
☐ swim	☐ trip	☐ reade
☐ fealings	☐ crayon	☐ two
☐ brave	☐ pencil	☐ four
☐ unhappy	☐ pen	☐ five
☐ upset	☐ papper	☐ eght
☐ garden	☐ north	☐ ship
☐ farm	☐ soth	☐ ocean
☐ chiken	☐ east	☐ floot
☐ ranch	☐ west	☐ captain
☐ clok	☐ morning	☐ dish
☐ time	☐ afternon	☐ plate
☐ minute	☐ evening	☐ spoon
☐ hour	☐ night	☐ dinnar

©2008 Plutarch Publications, Inc. PPI-1002

Name _____   Standard: Blends

Say the name of the item in the picture. Put an **X** in the box next to the blend that you hear when you name the picture.

	☐ NK ☐ TH ☐ MP ☐ NG		☐ FL ☐ CR ☐ SK ☐ WH
	☐ CH ☐ BR ☐ SC ☐ SL		☐ CK ☐ NK ☐ NG ☐ PH
	☐ GL ☐ FR ☐ FL ☐ SM		☐ SL ☐ NK ☐ KN ☐ DR
	☐ SM ☐ SN ☐ SP ☐ SW		☐ PL ☐ FR ☐ SP ☐ SH
12	☐ ND ☐ ST ☐ TR ☐ TW	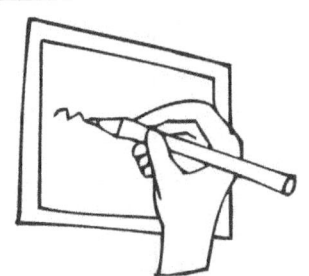	☐ WR ☐ PL ☐ MP ☐ CH

Name _____   Standard: Blends

Say the name of the item in the picture. Put an **X** in the box next to the blend that you hear when you name the picture.

(bench)	☐ TH ☐ PH ☐ CH ☐ CK	(nest)	☐ NK ☐ ST ☐ NG ☐ TH
(strawberry)	☐ STR ☐ BL ☐ GL ☐ SK	(tree)	☐ SN ☐ CR ☐ TR ☐ WH
(smoke)	☐ SC ☐ SK ☐ SN ☐ SM	(fly)	☐ PH ☐ FL ☐ FR ☐ CL
(steps)	☐ ST ☐ SP ☐ TH ☐ SM	(swing)	☐ CK ☐ CL ☐ SW ☐ BR
(thumb)	☐ PH ☐ DR ☐ GL ☐ TH	(shell)	☐ GR ☐ SH ☐ PL ☐ KN

©2008 Plutarch Publications, Inc. PPI-1002

Name _____   Standard: Blends

Say the name of the item in the picture. Put an **X** in the box next to the blend that you hear when you name the picture.

(teeth)	☐ TR ☐ TH ☐ PH ☐ DR		(train)	☐ TW ☐ SM ☐ TR ☐ CH	
(wheel)	☐ WH ☐ PL ☐ SH ☐ WR		(bed)	☐ SN ☐ KN ☐ BR ☐ BL	
(chair)	☐ TH ☐ CH ☐ PR ☐ GR		(cloud)	☐ PH ☐ CL ☐ CK ☐ FR	
(flower)	☐ WH ☐ BL ☐ SP ☐ FL		(glass)	☐ GL ☐ GR ☐ ST ☐ SK	
(knife)	☐ KN ☐ SN ☐ NK ☐ PH		(wing)	☐ KN ☐ SN ☐ NK ☐ NG	

©2008 Plutarch Publications, Inc. PPI -1002

Name _____   Standard: Blends

Say the name of the item in the picture. Put an **X** in the box next to the blend that you hear when you name the picture.

Picture	Blends	Picture	Blends
(bread)	☐ GR ☐ BL ☐ TW ☐ BR	(lock)	☐ TW ☐ CK ☐ FL ☐ PH
(watch)	☐ WH ☐ NK ☐ PL ☐ CH	(grapes)	☐ GR ☐ GL ☐ NG ☐ SH
(phone)	☐ PH ☐ TH ☐ NK ☐ DR	(plane)	☐ SK ☐ CH ☐ SM ☐ PL
(present)	☐ PL ☐ PR ☐ PH ☐ TR	(scarf)	☐ TW ☐ BR ☐ SC ☐ SW
(mask)	☐ SK ☐ SP ☐ SL ☐ SN	(band)	☐ TH ☐ NG ☐ ND ☐ MP

©2008 Plutarch Publications, Inc. PPI-1002

Name _____   Standard: Vowels

Read each word and listen to the sound of the letters that are underlined. Put and **X** in the box next to the word that has the same sound as the underlined letters.

1. gr<u>ow</u>	☐ cow ☐ coat ☐ flood		2. br<u>a</u>ce	☐ carry ☐ gather ☐ lady
3. m<u>u</u>sic	☐ rule ☐ upset ☐ touch		4. l<u>i</u>ck	☐ size ☐ sight ☐ silly
5. m<u>u</u>d	☐ true ☐ summer ☐ fruit		6. <u>a</u>gree	☐ able ☐ idea ☐ lean
7. m<u>oa</u>n	☐ own ☐ won ☐ prove		8. ch<u>ie</u>f	☐ blew ☐ neck ☐ either
9. y<u>a</u>rd	☐ wake ☐ raise ☐ farm		10. w<u>i</u>tch	☐ quiet ☐ quilt ☐ nine
11. f<u>oo</u>d	☐ moon ☐ trot ☐ join		12. m<u>ou</u>th	☐ some ☐ low ☐ south

©2008 PLUTARCH PUBLICATIONS, INC. PPI-1002

Name _____   Standard: Vowels

Read each word and listen to the sound of the letters that are underlined. Put and **X** in the box next to the word that has the same sound as the underlined letters.

1. tr<u>u</u>th	☐ funny ☐ flute ☐ aunt	2. p<u>o</u>ny	☐ rose ☐ month ☐ done
3. c<u>a</u>ge	☐ nap ☐ smart ☐ plate	4. str<u>aw</u>	☐ sail ☐ strange ☐ draw
5. br<u>o</u>ke	☐ blow ☐ done ☐ loud	6. qu<u>i</u>ck	☐ string ☐ tight ☐ piece
7. tr<u>u</u>nk	☐ burn ☐ pump ☐ four	8. fr<u>ee</u>	☐ held ☐ earth ☐ meat
9. fr<u>i</u>ghten	☐ pipe ☐ visit ☐ milk	10. cr<u>a</u>b	☐ share ☐ trap ☐ warm
11. sp<u>oo</u>n	☐ good ☐ indoor ☐ fool	12. b<u>ur</u>n	☐ stair ☐ fur ☐ drum

©2008 PLUTARCH PUBLICATIONS, INC. PPI-1002

Name _____   Standard: Vowels

Read each word and listen to the sound of the letters that are underlined. Put and **X** in the box next to the word that has the same sound as the underlined letters.

1. kn<u>i</u>fe	☐ flip ☐ dirt ☐ fight	2. sh<u>ar</u>p	☐ clay ☐ chair ☐ smart
3. l<u>oo</u>se	☐ look ☐ school ☐ foot	4. cl<u>ow</u>n	☐ low ☐ lock ☐ town
5. l<u>u</u>nch	☐ music ☐ dug ☐ blue	6. c<u>oi</u>n	☐ joy ☐ cool ☐ monkey
7. cl<u>ue</u>	☐ hunt ☐ June ☐ dust	8. d<u>ir</u>t	☐ bright ☐ drive ☐ bird
9. pl<u>a</u>nt	☐ band ☐ bake ☐ hair	10. d<u>i</u>sh	☐ prince ☐ ice ☐ five
11. h<u>u</u>ng	☐ Tuesday ☐ yourself ☐ rush	12. l<u>o</u>ck	☐ snow ☐ shot ☐ pool

©2008 Plutarch Publications, Inc. PPI -1002

Name _____   Standard: Vowels

Read each word and listen to the sound of the letters that are underlined. Put and **X** in the box next to the word that has the same sound as the underlined letters.

1. sk<u>a</u>te	☐ machine ☐ taste ☐ candy	2. thr<u>ew</u>	☐ weed ☐ scream ☐ root
3. dr<u>u</u>m	☐ hunt ☐ moon ☐ hour	4. d<u>e</u>sk	☐ sheet ☐ teach ☐ net
5. l<u>ie</u>	☐ sigh ☐ pink ☐ met	6. sh<u>ow</u>	☐ now ☐ hope ☐ done
7. h<u>u</u>nt	☐ thumb ☐ four ☐ huge	8. sm<u>ar</u>t	☐ pair ☐ salt ☐ yard
9. sh<u>or</u>t	☐ moan ☐ porch ☐ patch	10. c<u>au</u>ght	☐ walk ☐ enough ☐ warm
11. ind<u>ee</u>d	☐ beat ☐ belt ☐ feather	12. bl<u>a</u>nket	☐ mark ☐ grade ☐ cap

Name _____   Standard: Context Clues

Put an **X** in the box beside the word that best completes each sentence.

1. A good place to bend your leg is at the _____.
   ☐ join   ☐ knee   ☐ climb

2. Something we drink at a meal is _____.
   ☐ milk   ☐ bottle   ☐ mud

3. The birds used _____ to build their nest.
   ☐ outdoor   ☐ worms   ☐ twigs

4. I _____ a letter to Alyssa.
   ☐ wrote   ☐ shut   ☐ paint

5. Joel lives in the city and Frank lives on a _____.
   ☐ ladder   ☐ bench   ☐ farm

6. Jessie's _____ color is blue.
   ☐ favorite   ☐ send   ☐ wire

7. Please be _____ when you cross the street.
   ☐ signal   ☐ careful   ☐ peek

8. Today we _____ facts about our country.
   ☐ learned   ☐ cannot   ☐ almost

9. It is my turn to take out the _____.
   ☐ mind   ☐ garbage   ☐ garage

10. The _____ in the zoo made us laugh.
    ☐ corn   ☐ silver   ☐ monkey

Name _____   Standard: Context Clues

Put an **X** in the box beside the word that best completes each sentence.

1. Three ducks were swimming on the _____.
   - ☐ **pond** ☐ **ice** ☐ **vine**

2. Let's _____ we are asleep!
   - ☐ **pretend** ☐ **wave** ☐ **magic**

3. The bunny was eating a _____.
   - ☐ **bend** ☐ **jam** ☐ **carrot**

4. I think I saw a _____ under my bed!
   - ☐ **middle** ☐ **monster** ☐ **held**

5. I would like to _____ my shoes before we go.
   - ☐ **change** ☐ **leap** ☐ **easy**

6. Did Allen _____ you to his party?
   - ☐ **fool** ☐ **meet** ☐ **invite**

7. Cars are made in a big _____.
   - ☐ **mirror** ☐ **factory** ☐ **collect**

8. Pam took the _____ to the second floor.
   - ☐ **mine** ☐ **elevator** ☐ **free**

9. Are you _____ when you are by yourself?
   - ☐ **lonely** ☐ **happen** ☐ **button**

10. Use the _____ to cross the river.
    - ☐ **belong** ☐ **forest** ☐ **bridge**

Name _____   Standard: Context Clues

Read each sentence. Put an **X** in the box beside the word that **DOES NOT** make sense in the sentence.

1. Sylvia has a _____ dress.
   ☐ green   ☐ pretty   ☐ spent

2. We went to the library in the _____ .
   ☐ before   ☐ afternoon   ☐ morning

3. Our class listened to the _____ for one hour.
   ☐ music   ☐ heavy   ☐ story

4. Help me put the _____ on the bed.
   ☐ knew   ☐ blanket   ☐ sheet

5. Ken has _____ in his lunch today.
   ☐ cheese   ☐ hide   ☐ fruit

6. Jack will wear a red _____ with those pants.
   ☐ belt   ☐ grab   ☐ shirt

7. Put the flowers in the _____ of the table.
   ☐ hammer   ☐ center   ☐ middle

8. It will cost one _____ for a piece of gum.
   ☐ press   ☐ penny   ☐ dime

9. The _____ sat on the throne.
   ☐ queen   ☐ prince   ☐ both

10. Brian will play _____ today.
    ☐ indoors   ☐ beyond   ☐ outdoors

©2008 Plutarch Publications, Inc. PPI-1002

Name _____   Standard: Context Clues

Read each sentence. Put an **X** in the box beside the word that **DOES NOT** make sense in the sentence.

1. Shelia brought her lunch in a _____ today.
   ☐ basket   ☐ honey   ☐ sack

2. Ned used _____ to color the picture.
   ☐ bumps   ☐ crayons   ☐ paints

3. My teacher reads a _____ every day.
   ☐ newspaper   ☐ edge   ☐ map

4. I will eat _____ at the movie.
   ☐ wool   ☐ popcorn   ☐ candy

5. The _____ is a part of a plant.
   ☐ root   ☐ leaf   ☐ finger

6. Will _____ help me with this problem?
   ☐ somebody   ☐ anybody   ☐ anymore

7. Sara fell and hurt her _____.
   ☐ weather   ☐ shoulder   ☐ arm

8. My family took a trip to the _____ this summer.
   ☐ ocean   ☐ beach   ☐ evening

9. Ted got the lemon from the _____.
   ☐ crawl   ☐ kitchen   ☐ market

10. There was a _____ in front of the house.
    ☐ fence   ☐ smooth   ☐ sidewalk

Name _____   Standard: Sequence of Events

Sequence means to put things in order. For each group below, number the items in the order given.

Youngest to Oldest:
_____ child
_____ grandparent
_____ teenager
_____ baby
_____ toddler
_____ parent

Small to Large:
_____ beachball
_____ baseball
_____ pea
_____ golf ball
_____ basketball
_____ planet

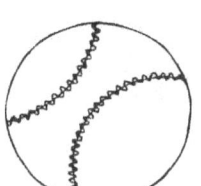

Light to Heavy:
_____ elephant
_____ snail
_____ rabbit
_____ frog
_____ horse
_____ dog

Least to Most:
_____ dime
_____ penny
_____ quarter
_____ dollar
_____ nickel
_____ half dollar

Shortest to Longest:
_____ month
_____ day
_____ week
_____ minute
_____ year
_____ hour

A to Z:
_____ strawberry
_____ peach
_____ apple
_____ grapes
_____ banana
_____ watermelon

©2008 Plutarch Publications, Inc. PPI-1002

Name _____   Standard: Sequence of Events

Sequence of Events is the order in which things happen. Below are things we see or do each day. Number them in order from first to last, just as they should happen.

My Day:

_____ I eat my breakfast.

_____ I work and play at school.

_____ I wake up.

_____ The bus brings me home.

_____ I eat my dinner.

_____ I get out of bed.

_____ The bus takes me to school.

_____ I go to bed.

Make a Cake:

_____ Buy a cake mix.

_____ Pour the batter into a pan.

_____ Bake until it is finished.

_____ Add eggs and milk to the mix.

_____ Get out the bowl and spoon.

_____ Stir until it's well mixed.

_____ Put the mix in the bowl.

_____ Put the pan in the oven.

Buying Gum:

_____ Pick up your package.

_____ Get your change back.

_____ Choose the gum you like.

_____ Look at all the gum.

_____ Go to the store.

_____ Leave the store.

_____ Pay the cashier.

_____ Get in line to check out.

Wash Your Face:

_____ Wet the washcloth.

_____ Wash your face.

_____ Rinse your face.

_____ Dry your face.

_____ Rinse soap off the washcloth.

_____ Put soap on the washcloth.

_____ Turn on the water.

_____ Turn off the water.

©2008 Plutarch Publications, Inc. PPI-1002

Name _____   Standard: Sequence of Events

Read the story.

Randy's Garden

Randy wanted a garden in his backyard. First he dug up the grass. Next he hoed the dirt until it was loose. Then he planted a row of carrot seeds. After that he planted a row of lettuce seeds. Finally he planted a row of tomato seedlings. What a good garden!

Read these sentences.

He planted carrots in the first row.

The last things planted were tomato seedlings.

Randy used a hoe to loosen the dirt.

Randy dug up the grass.

Next, lettuce seeds were planted.

On the lines below, write the sentences in order as they happened in the story.

1. _____

2. _____

3. _____

4. _____

5. _____

©2008 Plutarch Publications, Inc. PPI -1002

Name _____   Standard: Fact or Opinion

A **FACT** is something that is real and can be proven.
An **OPINION** is a belief or the way you feel about something.

Read the statements below. Decide if each is a fact or an opinion. On the blank, write **F** if it is fact and **O** if it is opinion.

_____ 1. There are twenty-four hours in every day.
_____ 2. We should use more hours for playing than for working.
_____ 3. Each day has a morning, afternoon, evening, and night.
_____ 4. Afternoons are more fun than mornings.
_____ 5. Six o'clock is the very best time to eat dinner.
_____ 6. The sun rises in the morning and sets in the evening.
_____ 7. Stars can be seen in the night sky.
_____ 8. The moon is beautiful to look at.
_____ 9. There are seven days in a week.
_____ 10. One week is a long time.
_____ 11. Monday is the worst day of the week.
_____ 12. Saturday is the best day of the week.
_____ 13. Wednesday is a hard word to spell!
_____ 14. Thursday is the day before Friday.
_____ 15. Sunday is always a good day for a picnic.
_____ 16. Tuesday is the day before Wednesday.
_____ 17. A week of summer is more fun than a week of winter.
_____ 18. There are 30 or 31 days in every month except February.
_____ 19. There are twelve months in a year.
_____ 20. October is the best month because it has Halloween!

Write one fact and one opinion about any month you choose.
Fact: _____
Opinion: _____

©2008 Plutarch Publications, Inc. PPI-1002

Name _____   Standard: Fact or Opinion

> A **FACT** is something that is real and can be proven.
> An **OPINION** is a belief or the way you feel about something.

Read the statements below. Decide if each is a fact or an opinion. On the blank, write **F** if it is fact and **O** if it is opinion.

_____ 1. Fruit comes from plants.
_____ 2. Oranges and lemons are the best kind of fruit.
_____ 3. Lemons are prettier because they are yellow.
_____ 4. Oranges and lemons grow on trees.
_____ 5. The flowers on the orange tree smell better than roses!
_____ 6. Strawberries and blueberries are fruit.
_____ 7. Strawberries are red.
_____ 8. Blueberries taste best in a pie.
_____ 9. Strawberry jam is better than blueberry jam.
_____ 10. Grapes can be red or green.
_____ 11. Red grapes are better than green grapes.
_____ 12. Grapes grow in bunches.
_____ 13. Grapes are dried to make raisins.
_____ 14. Apples are the best fruit of all!
_____ 15. Apples can be red, green, or yellow.
_____ 16. Apple pie is better than blueberry or lemon pie.
_____ 17. Apples grow on trees.
_____ 18. Fruit is a healthy food to eat.
_____ 19. The best snacks are made with fruit.
_____ 20. All fruit tastes great!

Write one fact and one opinion about any fruit you choose.

Fact: _____

Opinion: _____

©2008 Plutarch Publications, Inc. PPI-1002

Name _____   Standard: Fact or Opinion

> A **FACT** is something that is real and can be proven.
> An **OPINION** is a belief or the way you feel about something.

Read the statements below. Decide if each is a fact or an opinion. On the blank, write **F** if it is fact and **O** if it is opinion.

_____ 1. Dogs, cats, birds, and rabbits are common pets.
_____ 2. Large black dogs are the nicest pets.
_____ 3. Many people own dogs.
_____ 4. Small dogs are best because they can live indoors.
_____ 5. Dogs can bark and wag their tails.
_____ 6. Some dogs have long fur.
_____ 7. Girls think cats are better than dogs.
_____ 8. Cats meow.
_____ 9. Cats are sneaky and mean.
_____ 10. All cats are mean to dogs and mice.
_____ 11. Pet birds often live in cages.
_____ 12. Birds are noisy and not nice pets.
_____ 13. Some people have parrots as pets.
_____ 14. Birds are beautiful and fun to watch.
_____ 15. Rabbits are the cutest pets because they have long ears!
_____ 16. Rabbits hop and eat lettuce.
_____ 17. Rabbits do not make good pets.
_____ 18. Birds are nicer than rabbits and cats.
_____ 19. The best pets of all are fish.
_____ 20. Dogs, cats, birds, and rabbits make the best pets.

Write one fact and one opinion about a pet you choose.

Fact: _____

_____

Opinion: _____

_____

©2008 Plutarch Publications, Inc. PPI-1002

Name _____   Standard: Compare/Contrast

We **compare** and **contrast** things to find out
how they are **alike** and how they are **different**.

button

basketball

Read each statement below. If the statement describes the button, write **X** on the line. If the statement describes the basketball, write **O** on the line. If the statement describes both items, write **B** on the line.

_____ 1. I am round.
_____ 2. You can play with me.
_____ 3. I am full of air.
_____ 4. I can roll.
_____ 5. You find me on clothes.
_____ 6. Many people like to play games with me.
_____ 7. You can sew me on things.
_____ 8. I help keep things closed.
_____ 9. I go through something.
_____ 10. You can bounce me.
_____ 11. I have holes in me.
_____ 12. I am the bigger item.
_____ 13. I am the smaller item.
_____ 14. People use me.
_____ 15. You can buy me in a store.

©2008 Plutarch Publications, Inc. PPI-1002

Name _____

Standard: Compare/Contrast

We **compare** and **contrast** things to find out how they are **alike** and how they are **different**.

roller skates

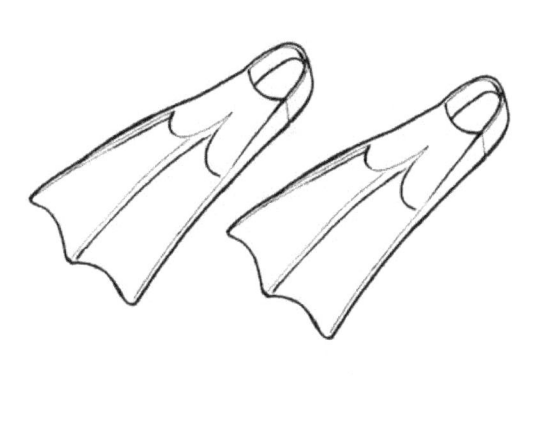

swim fins

Read each statement below. If the statement describes the skates, write **X** on the line. If the statement describes the swim fins write **O** on the line. If the statement describes both items, write **B** on the line.

_____ 1. I am used in the water.

_____ 2. I have wheels.

_____ 3. I help you move faster.

_____ 4. I make you move like a fish.

_____ 5. You put me on your feet.

_____ 6. I have laces that tie.

_____ 7. I make your feet feel much longer than they really are.

_____ 8. I am used when you are playing.

_____ 9. You might find me at the beach.

_____ 10. I help people exercise.

_____ 11. I can be fun to use!

_____ 12. You should wear a helmet when you use me.

_____ 13. I like to get wet.

_____ 14. I am used on sidewalks and in parks.

_____ 15. I am used for sports.

©2008 Plutarch Publications, Inc. PPI -1002

Name _____   Standard: Compare/Contrast

We **compare** and **contrast** things to find out
how they are **alike** and how they are **different**.

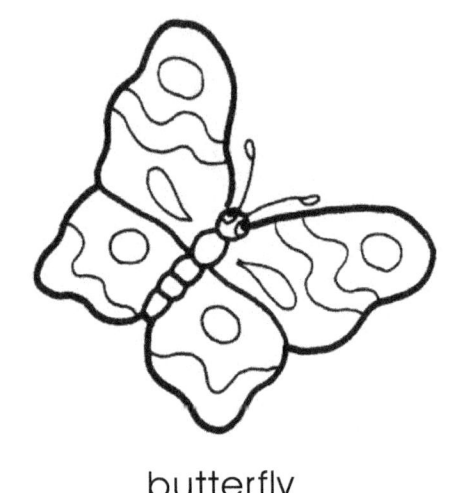
butterfly

bird

Read each statement below. If the statement describes the butterfly, write **X** on the line. If the statement describes the bird, write **O** on the line. If the statement describes both items, write **B** on the line.

_____ 1. I can fly.
_____ 2. I have a tail and a beak.
_____ 3. I have wings.
_____ 4. I have feathers.
_____ 5. I like to eat worms.
_____ 6. I have six legs.
_____ 7. I lay eggs.
_____ 8. I was once a caterpillar.
_____ 9. I live outdoors.
_____ 10. Many people think I am beautiful.
_____ 11. I like to be near flowers.
_____ 12. I can float on the wind.
_____ 13. I make a sound like a whistle.
_____ 14. I make no sound at all.
_____ 15. I live in a nest.

Name _____   Standard: Story Elements

Story Elements:
Title: the name of the book
Author: the person who wrote the story
Illustrator: the person who drew the pictures for the book
Characters: the people or things about whom the story is told
Plot: the events that happen in the story
Setting: when and where the story takes place

Read the statements below. On the line write **T** if the statement is about the title, **A** for author, **I** for illustrator, **C** for characters, **P** for plot, or **S** for setting.

_____ 1. *James and the Giant Peach* is a very good book.

_____ 2. This story is about a boy named James Henry Trotter.

_____ 3. The pictures by Nancy Ekholm Burkert are beautiful!

_____ 4. The story takes place in England and New York.

_____ 5. James lives with his two mean aunts who do not like him.

_____ 6. Roald Dahl wrote this story.

_____ 7. A spilled bag of magic green things makes a giant peach grow on the old peach tree during the night.

_____ 8. James has many adventures with a group of giant insects.

_____ 9. Ladybug is very kind to James.

_____ 10. Grasshopper plays music with his wings and legs.

_____ 11. The peach rolls to the ocean and sharks try to eat it.

_____ 12. Birds fly the peach to New York.

_____ 13. Centipede tells silly stories and is funny.

_____ 14. The peach lands on the Empire State Building.

_____ 15. Henry and his friends end up living in New York.

©2008 PLUTARCH PUBLICATIONS, INC. PPI-1002

Name _____   Standard: Story Elements

Story Elements:
Title: the name of the book
Author: the person who wrote the story
Illustrator: the person who drew the pictures for the book
Characters: the people or things about whom the story is told
Plot: the events that happen in the story
Setting: when and where the story takes place

Read the statements below. On the line write **T** if the statement is about the title, **A** for author, **I** for illustrator, **C** for characters, **P** for plot, or **S** for setting.

_____ 1. A good book to read is *The Very Quiet Cricket.*

_____ 2. The story is about a young cricket.

_____ 3. The story takes place in a field.

_____ 4. The cricket does not know how to make noise with his wings.

_____ 5. Different insects say hello, but the cricket cannot answer.

_____ 6. The pictures by Eric Carle are painted on glass.

_____ 7. The little cricket keeps rubbing his wings together, but he cannot make a sound.

_____ 8. A locust and dragonfly are two of the animals in the book.

_____ 9. The bumblebee buzzes.

_____ 10. A beautiful luna moth flys by at night.

_____ 11. The cricket is sad because he cannot chirp.

_____ 12. The cricket meets another quiet little cricket.

_____ 13. The very quiet cricket rubs his wings once more and chirps!

_____ 14. The chirp is the most beautiful sound they have ever heard.

_____ 15. Eric Carle wrote this and many other books.

©2008 Plutarch Publications, Inc. PPI -1002

Name _____   (Standard: Story Elements)

A book report tells about all the story elements. Choose your favorite book and use this book report to tell about it.

Title of the book: _____
_____

Author: _____

Illustrator: _____

Characters: _____
_____
_____

Setting: _____
_____

Plot: _____
_____
_____
_____
_____
_____
_____

Things I liked about the book: _____
_____

Things I didn't like about the book: _____
_____

©2008 Plutarch Publications, Inc. PPI-1002

Name _____ Standard: Genre

> **Genre** is the style in which a story is written. Two types of genre are:
> **Fiction** - a story that has been made up and didn't really happen
> **Nonfiction** - a story about people or events that are real

Read the statements below. On the line write **F** if the book is fiction (made up). Write **N** if it the book is nonfiction (about a real person or event).

_____ 1. *Amelia Bedelia Goes Camping*, by Peggy Parish, is a story about silly Amelia who mixes up the meaning of words. When she is told to pitch a tent, she throws it into a bush!

_____ 2. Learn about the tracks that different animals leave in the mud and snow in *Animal Tracks*, a book by Arthur Dorros.

_____ 3. *Nine True Dolphin Stories* by Margaret Davidson. This book gives facts about dolphins and their human friends.

_____ 4. In the book *Danny and the Dinosaur* by Syd Hoff, a boy goes to a museum where a friendly dinosaur comes to life and they play together.

_____ 5. Learn what it means to be true friends in the book *Frog and Toad are Friends* by Arnold Lobel. Toad helps Frog feel better when he is sick. Frog writes a letter to Toad when Toad is sad because he has no mail.

_____ 6. *Skeletons! Skeletons!* by Katy Hall tells about the bones in our bodies.

_____ 7. Find out how milk is made and how it gets to the store in the book *Milk Makers* by Gail Gibbons.

_____ 8. *Morris Goes to School* by B. Wiseman, is a story about a moose who goes to school to learn to read and count.

©2008 Plutarch Publications, Inc. PPI -1002

Name _____ Standard: Narrative Comprehension

Juan likes to ride his bike. He rides it to school. He rides it to the store. He rides it around town! Juan is very fast on his bike. One day Juan was taking a ride with his friend, Pedro. They decided to have a race to see who was the faster rider. The race would begin at Pedro's driveway and end at the fence near the end of the block. The boys lined up their bikes. Ready, set, go! The boys sped down the sidewalk, each pushing hard on the pedals. Suddenly Juan saw a turtle crawling in his path. He slammed on the brakes and **skidded** to a stop. Pedro kept going and finally stopped at the fence. He turned around and rode back to Juan. Pedro declared that Juan was the winner, even though he did not finish the race. The two friends picked up the turtle and took it to the nearby creek where it would be safe from speeding bikes.

1. What are the names of the boys? _____
2. Where did the race begin? _____

Name three places Juan likes to ride his bike.

3. _____
4. _____
5. _____

6. Why did Juan stop during the race?
_____
_____

7. What word means almost the same as the word "skidded"?
   A. behind   B. slid   C. kicked

8. What would be a good title for this story?
   A. A Boy Named Pedro
   B. Juan and Pedro Race
   C. The Turtle

|  **Think about it:** What would you have done if you were Juan? |  **Draw it:** Draw a picture of Juan and the turtle. |

©2008 Plutarch Publications, Inc. PPI-1002

Name _____   Standard: Narrative Comprehension

Roxie, the dog, lay on the grass in the front yard of his house. He was **bored** because there was nothing to do. His owner, a boy named Jack, was at school so there wasn't anyone to play with. Roxie looked up and down the street but there wasn't a person in sight. A butterfly was flitting around the flower bed. Roxie stood up and walked to the flowers. The butterfly fluttered nearer and nearer until it landed right on Roxie's nose! Roxie stood still, waiting for the butterfly to move. Finally it flew back to the flowers. Roxie wagged his tail and barked. He wanted to play. The butterfly quickly flew away. Roxie was sad that his new friend was gone. He heard footsteps coming up the sidewalk. It was his boy coming home from school. Now Roxie was happy.

1. What is the name of the dog in the story? _____
2. Where was the dog? _____

Name three things the dog did in this story.

3. _____
4. _____
5. _____

6. Why was the dog happy at the end of the story?

_____
_____

7. What does the word "bored" mean?

    A. excited   B. angry   C. have nothing to do

8. What would be a good title for this story?
   A. Jack and His Dog
   B. The Butterfly
   C. Roxie Wants to Play

 **Look for it:** Find a picture of a butterfly.

 **Play it:** Pretend you are a butterfly. Let your arms be your wings and "fly".

©2008 Plutarch Publications, Inc. PPI -1002

Name _____   Standard: Narrative Comprehension

Fluffy was a young bunny who lived in a nest under the ferns just beyond the flower garden. She had four sisters that lived in the nest with her. Their mother often left the nest to go find food, leaving the bunnies alone. Fluffy was **curious** about the world outside her nest. She had peeked out a few times, but had never stepped one paw past the door. The world outside looked bright and Fluffy was tired of the dark nest. One day while Mother was out, Fluffy bravely hopped into the patch of ferns. It felt good to be in the fresh air, so she jumped and wiggled with joy. She **nibbled** on a leaf and a piece of grass. What fun the world was! Suddenly Fluffy heard a dog bark. She ran back to her nest and snuggled with her sisters. The nest was the best place to be!

1. Who is the main character in this story? _____
2. How many sisters does the bunny have? _____

Name three things Fluffy did outside the nest.

3. _____

4. _____

5. _____

6. What does the story mean when it says Fluffy was "curious"?

_____

_____

7. What does the word "nibble" mean?

   A. take a bite   B. sleep   C. go outside

8. What would be a good title for this story?

   A. Fluffy Leaves the Nest
   B. Five Bunnies in the Ferns
   C. Mother Rabbit Finds Food

 **Share it:** Tell a friend about a time when you did something brave.	 **Act it out:** Pretend you are Fluffy. Show how she left the nest and explored the world.

©2008 Plutarch Publications, Inc. PPI-1002

Name _____   Standard: Narrative Comprehension

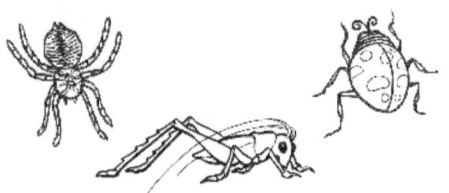

James has a **hobby** that he really enjoys. He collects bugs! When James was four years old he got an Ant Farm for his birthday. He loved watching the ants as they dug tunnels and built nests. At five years old, James had three jars of dirt. One was for spiders, another for grasshoppers, and the last held beetles he had found under a log. For his sixth birthday, James got a little cage that could hold all kinds of bugs. He likes to catch the bugs, put them in the cage, and watch them for a few days. He thinks it is interesting to see what they eat and how they build their homes. He has learned many things about these **insects** and likes to share them with his class at school. Not everyone likes bugs, but James sure does!

1. Who is the main character in this story? _____
2. What does this boy like to do? _____

Name three types of bugs that the boy has collected.

3. _____
4. _____
5. _____

6. What is a "hobby"?

_____

_____

7. What is another word for "insect"?

   A. nest   B. bug   C. hobby

8. What would be a good title for this story?

   A. The Life of Insects
   B. James Has a Hobby
   C. Our Ant Farm

 **Look for it:** See how many bugs you can find. Keep a list of their names.

 **Do it:** Start a collection of something you like. Tell the class about it.

Name _____   Standard: Narrative Comprehension

Tamika was very **excited**. It was her birthday and her parents had gotten tickets to Sea Kingdom, a park with **dolphins** and whales. Tamika's mom and dad knew that she loved dolphins and the show would be a great birthday present for her. Tamika found seats right in the front row of the stands! The music started and the show began. Tamika enjoyed watching the dolphins race across the pool and jump high into the air. They did flips and waved their fins at the people in the stands. The best surprise of all came when the dolphin trainers invited her to join them beside the pool. Tamika got to throw a ball to one of the dolphins, and the dolphin threw it back to her. At the end of the show, Tamika held out a treat and the dolphin took it right from her hand!

1. Who is the main character in this story? _____
2. Where was the character going? _____

   Name three things the dolphins did for the show.

3. _____
4. _____
5. _____

6. Why was this trip a good present to give to Tamika?

   _____
   _____

7. What means almost the same as the word "excited"?

   A. not feeling well   B. feeling sad   C. feeling happy

8. What would be a good title for this story?

   A. Tamika's Birthday Surprise
   B. The Dolphin Plays
   C. Tamika and Her Parents

 **Write about it:** What would you like to do on your birthday?

 **Think about it:** How are dolphins and whales alike?

Name _____   Standard: Narrative Comprehension

Once there were three little mice that lived in a nest under a bush in the park. This was a good home for the mice. It was warm and dry. It was soft because they had filled it with bits of cloth and paper they found in the park. The park was often visited by children who brought **delicious** things to eat, such as sandwiches, cake or candy. The mice would watch from the **safety** of their nest, where they couldn't be seen as children played during the day. At night the three mice would carefully tiptoe out of the nest and look for food and little treasures the children had left behind. The mice often found colorful ribbons and buttons, and at times they might find a coin. The mice were happy in their nest under the bush. It was a wonderful place for mice to live!

1. Who are the main characters in this story? _____
2. Where do they live? _____

Name three things the mice might find at night.

3. _____
4. _____
5. _____

6. Why was the nest a place of "safety" for the mice?
_____
_____

7. Which of these three things might be "delicious"?
   A. carrots   B. toys   C. boots

8. What would be a good title for this story?
   A. Cake and Candy
   B. Three Blind Mice
   C. A Home Under the Bush

 **Act it out:** Pretend to be a mouse. How would you move?

 Find it: Look in a newspaper to find words that describe a mouse.

©2008 Plutarch Publications, Inc. PPI-1002

Name _____   Standard: Narrative Comprehension

Padma takes piano lessons **twice**, or two times, every week. She practices every day because it helps her become a better player. It feels like magic when the music fills the room as her fingers hit those piano keys! Sometimes Padma does not feel like practicing. She would much rather go outside and play with her friends. But Padma has the dream of being in a famous **pianist** some day . She wants to walk across a stage, sit at a huge piano, and play beautiful music for a large group of people. She knows it will take a lot of hard work and practice to reach her dream. When Padma's fingers become tired during practice, she closes her eyes and pictures her dream. The dream makes her smile, and helps her to keep playing.

1. Who is the main character in this story? _____
2. What does she do every day? _____

Name three things that happen in Padma's dream.

3. _____

4. _____

5. _____

6. What is a "pianist"?

   _____

   _____

7. What does the word "twice" mean?

   A. every week   B. every day   C. two times

8. What would be a good title for this story?

   A. Padma Plays the Piano
   B. The Famous Piano
   C. Tired of Playing

 **Do it:** Find out how many people you know play the piano or other instruments.

 **Think about it:** What do you dream of becoming when you grow up?

Name _____ Standard: Narrative Comprehension

Poor Peter was not feeling very happy. His father was taking him to the **dentist** today. The dentist was going to clean and x-ray his teeth to see if he had a **cavity**, or hole, that needed to be filled. Peter carefully brushed his teeth and then went to the dentist's office. He sat in a large chair. The dentist put a paper apron around Peter's neck and then took three x-ray pictures of his teeth. Peter opened his mouth wide so the dentist could clean his teeth. When he was finished cleaning, the dentist showed Peter the x-rays. There were no cavities and the dentist said his teeth looked healthy. The dentist gave Peter a new toothbrush and a tube of toothpaste. Peter was happy that his visit to the dentist was finally over!

1. Who is the main character in this story? _____
2. Where was he going? _____

Name three things the dentist did.

3. _____
4. _____
5. _____
6. What is a "dentist"?

_____
_____

7. What does the word "cavity" mean?
   A. clean teeth   B. a hole   C. to fill a tooth

8. What would be a good title for this story?
   A. Too Many Cavities
   B. Peter and His Father
   C. Peter Goes to the Dentist

 **Share it:** Tell someone what happened on your last trip to the dentist.

 Compare it: Do you feel like Peter when you go to the dentist?

Name _____   Standard: Narrative Comprehension

Maria went to the movie **theater** with her two best friends, Carla and Gina. They each bought a big bag of popcorn, a candy bar, and a cold drink. The girls found seats near the front of the theater where they could see everything. Maria sat between her friends and they talked until the lights **dimmed** and the room became almost dark. The movie started and the girls ate popcorn while they watched. It was a funny movie and the girls laughed a lot. Gina laughed so hard she had tears in her eyes. Maria laughed so hard she spilled her popcorn all over her lap! When the movie was over, the girls agreed that it was the funniest movie they had ever seen. Maria was glad she and her friends had so much fun.

1. Who is the main character in this story? _____
2. Who are her best friends? _____

Name three things the girls bought.

3. _____
4. _____
5. _____

6. What happens when lights are "dimmed"?
   _____
   _____

7. What is a "theater"?
   A. popcorn   B. a store   C. a place for shows

8. What would be a good title for this story?
   A. Maria and the Popcorn
   B. Fun at the Theater
   C. Carla and Gina are Friends

 Find it: Look in the newspaper to see what movies are at your neighborhood theater.

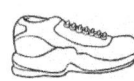 **Do it:** Pop some popcorn and watch a funny movie with your friends.

©2008 Plutarch Publications, Inc. PPI -1002

Name _____   Standard: Expository Comprehension

Living or Nonliving?

Sorting things into **categories**, or groups, can help us better understand the world. Everything you see is LIVING or NONLIVING. A person is living. A book is nonliving. Is a plant living? Yes, it is. There are seven characteristics (qualities) living things have but nonliving things do not. All living things can: 1) eat; 2) move; 3) grow; 4) **reproduce**, or have babies; 5) breathe; 6) remove waste; and 7) react to changes around them. It is easy to see how an animal is living, but a plant is harder to understand. Plants get food through their leaves and roots. They move by growing toward light. Plants are living things. Is jelly living or nonliving? Jelly is made from fruit. Fruit is part of a living plant, but jelly cannot eat or grow and it can't breathe or reproduce. Jelly is nonliving. All living things are either plants or animals.

Name the seven characteristics of living things.
1. _____
2. _____
3. _____
4. _____
5. _____
6. _____
7. _____

8. What is another word for "category"?

    A. living   B. group   C. person

Read the words. Write **L** if the item is living and **N** if it is nonliving.

____ 9. tree   ____ 10. horse   ____ 11. bread
____ 12. log   ____ 13. grass   ____ 14. ball
____ 15. lamp   ____ 16. rain   ____ 17. boat
____ 18. butterfly   ____ 19. ant   ____ 20. fish

Look for it: Look around your room. Make a list of six things that you can see. Tell if each one is living or nonliving.

Name _____   Standard: Expository Comprehension

Plants

Plants, although they do not move much, are living things. They eat food that they make from sunshine and water taken in through their roots and leaves. Plants **respire**, or "breathe" by taking in gases from the air. They **expel,** or get rid of, gases they don't use. When they get enough water and sunshine, plants will react by growing. When they don't get enough, they react by losing leaves, turning brown in spots, or dying. Most plants reproduce by making seeds. Some seeds are **produced** (made) in the flower of plants such trees, vegetables, and grass. Plants such as pine trees and tulips produce seeds in a cone or bulb. Ferns and some seaweeds produce spores, another type of seed. Plants are important to people and other animals. Much of the food we eat comes from plants. Also, a lot of the medicines we take comes from plants.

1. What is the title of this story? _____
2. What does the word "respire" mean? _____

Name three things that prove a plant is a living thing.

3. _____

4. _____

5. _____

6. What is another word for "produce"?

    A. make   B. die   C. grow

7. How do most plants reproduce? _____
8. What does the word "expel" mean? _____

Read the words. Write **P** if the food comes from a plant and **A** if it comes from an animal.

____ 9. beans   ____ 10. corn   ____ 11. milk

____ 12. bread   ____ 13. egg   ____ 14. peas

____ 15. carrot   ____ 16. ham   ____ 17. potato

____ 18. cheese   ____ 19. meat   ____ 20. rice

 Find it: Look in the newspaper for grocery store ads. Make a list of the foods advertised. Decide if they are foods from plants or animals.

©2008 PLUTARCH PUBLICATIONS, Inc. PPI -1002

Name _____   Standard: Expository Comprehension

Animals

Animals are living things. Just like plants, they eat, grow, breathe, and reproduce. However, animals can move about easily while plants hardly move at all. Animals can walk, fly, crawl, run, hop, skip, trot, and roll. Animals react with the world around them by using their **senses** of sight, hearing, smell, taste, and touch. Animals come in all shapes and sizes. Dinosaurs and **humans** (people) are animals, and so are bugs and worms. There are even some animals that are too tiny to see without a microscope! With so many types of animals, it was difficult to understand much about them. **Aristotle**, a man who lived over two thousand years ago, helped solve this problem by sorting all animals into categories. He grouped them by the things they had **in common**, or shared.

1. What is this story about?_____
2. What do animals do easily that plants can hardly do? _____

Name three of the five senses listed in the story.

3. _____
4. _____
5. _____

6. What is another word for "human"?

   A. animal   B. sense   C. person

7. What does a microscope do?_____
8. What does the phrase "in common" mean? _____

Which sense would be used for each item below? On the blank, write **S** for SIGHT or **H** for HEARING.

_____ 9. a butterfly   _____ 10. singing   _____ 11. music
_____ 12. a car horn   _____ 13. reading   _____ 14. snoring
_____ 15. a voice   _____ 16. a picture   _____ 17. goldfish
_____ 18. clouds   _____ 19. a doorbell   _____ 20. a plant

Make it: Start a scrapbook of animals. Find pictures of the animals you like and paste them in your book. Label them.

Name _____

Standard: Expository Comprehension

Mammals

It is easier to understand animals if they are sorted into groups or **classes**. The class that has the most animals is called mammals. Mammals can be as small as two inches, like the shrew which is a type of mole. They can also be as large as 100 feet long, like the blue whale. Some mammals walk on two legs, others walk on four legs, some have no legs, and some even fly! What makes mammals different from other animals? They have several common characteristics that all mammals share: 1) Mammals have a **spine**, or backbone; 2) Their bodies are covered with fur or hair; 3) They produce milk to feed their young; 4) Mammals give birth to live babies; and 5) Mammals are **warm-blooded** which means they make their own body heat. Humans are in this class of animals called mammals.

Name the five characteristics of mammals.

1. _____
2. _____
3. _____
4. _____
5. _____

6. Which word means the animal can make its own heat?

    A. mammal   B. spine   C. warm-blooded

7. What is another word for "group"? _____
8. What is another word for "backbone"? _____

Use the five characteristics of a mammal to decide if the animals below are mammals. Write **M** if it is a mammal and **N** if it is not.

_____ 9. frog   _____ 10. goat   _____ 11. fish

_____ 12. dog   _____ 13. snake   _____ 14. rabbit

_____ 15. deer   _____ 16. spider   _____ 17. cat

_____ 18. raccoon   _____ 19. ant   _____ 20. bee

Do it: Time yourself and a friend. See how many mammals each of you can list in ten minutes. Compare your lists. How many mammals did you list in all?

©2008 Plutarch Publications, Inc. PPI -1002

Name _____   Standard: Expository Comprehension

Birds

The class of animals known as birds can be found anywhere on Earth, from jungles to the ice caps at the north pole. Birds are not difficult to tell apart from most other animals. They have two characteristics that are the same as mammals: 1) All birds have a spine; and 2) They are warm-blooded. Birds have five other characteristics that make them very different from other animals: 3) Birds are covered with feathers; 4) They have a bill, or beak, but no teeth; 5) Not all birds can fly, but all of them do have wings; 6) Birds lay eggs and keep them warm until the babies are big enough to **hatch**, or break out on their own; and 7) Birds have a **wishbone** in their chest. This wishbone bends in to allow the bird to flap its wings. It also pushes out to keep the wings from crushing the chest.

Name the seven characteristics of birds.
1. _____
2. _____
3. _____
4. _____
5. _____
6. _____
7. _____

8. Which word means "to come out of an egg"?

    A. hatch   B. wishbone   C. jungle

Write **B** if the word is a characteristic of birds. Write **N** if it is not.

_____ 9. wings   _____ 10. live birth   _____ 11. spine

_____ 12. fins   _____ 13. feathers   _____ 14. hair

_____ 15. teeth   _____ 16. wishbone   _____ 17. fur

_____ 18. warm blooded   _____ 19. beak   _____ 20. eggs

Look for it: Go for a walk or look out your window and keep a count of how many birds you see. Find a book on birds and find what kind they are. Any crows? Robins? Herons?

Name _____

Standard: Expository Comprehension

Fish

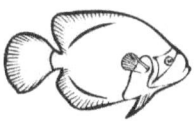

Fish are a class of animals that live in water all around the world. They can be found in ponds, rivers, lakes, oceans, fresh water, and salt water. Fish have seven characteristics, two of which are like mammals or birds: 1) Fish have spines like mammals and birds; 2) Most fish lay eggs, just like birds, but some fish do give birth to live babies, just like mammals; 3) Their bodies are covered with scales; 4) Fish live their whole lives in water; 5) They have **fins** instead of arms or legs; 6) Fish have gills, a special body part, that takes the air from the water so they can breathe; and 7) Fish cannot make their own heat, so they are cold-blooded. They get heat from the water where they live or by sitting where the sun shines on them. As the water warms or cools, the fish get warmer or colder as well.

Name the seven characteristics of fish.

1. _____
2. _____
3. _____
4. _____
5. _____
6. _____
7. _____
8. What do fish have instead of arms or legs? _____

Read the words below. Write **F** if the word is a characteristic of fish. Write **N** if it is not.

____ 9. warm-blooded   ____ 10. beak   ____ 11. fins
____ 12. scales   ____ 13. hair   ____ 14. spine
____ 15. live in water ____ 16. feathers   ____ 17. lay eggs
____ 18. live on land   ____ 19. cold-blooded ____ 20. gills

Compare it: Think about how different animals move. Make a list of animals that swim, fly, walk, and slide. Some animals may move in more than one way!

©2008 Plutarch Publications, Inc. PPI-1002

Name _____   Standard: Expository Comprehension

Reptiles

Reptiles are a class of animals that usually live on land, but often are very close to the water. This class includes snakes, turtles, lizards, crocodiles, alligators and other animals that are now **extinct** (died out) like the dinosaurs. Reptiles have some of the same characteristics of mammals and fish but a few things make them different: 1) Reptiles have a spine; 2) Like fish, they are cold-blooded; 3) Reptiles lay eggs in nests on land, like birds, but they do not take care of the young; 4) The skin of reptiles is dry and covered with small scales; 5) Reptiles have claws on their toes unless they do not have legs, like a snake or lizard without legs; and 6) Although reptiles may spend a lot of time in water they have lungs for breathing, just like mammals.

Name the six characteristics of reptiles.

1. _____
2. _____
3. _____
4. _____
5. _____
6. _____

Name two characteristics that birds and reptiles share:

7. _____
8. _____

Read the words. Write **R** if the animal is a reptile and **N** if it is not.

_____ 9. box turtle   _____ 10. rattle snake   _____ 11. gecko
_____ 12. goldfish   _____ 13. beaver   _____ 14. mouse
_____ 15. Komodo dragon   _____ 16. tortoise   _____ 17. fly
_____ 18. snail   _____ 19. alligator   _____ 20. bat

Think about it: Dinosaurs were reptiles. Which reptile that exists today is most like the dinosaur? Which characteristics do they share?

©2008 Plutarch Publications, Inc. PPI -1002

Name _____   Standard: Expository Comprehension

Amphibians

The word amphibian means "double life". Most amphibians spend half of their lives in water and the other half on land. Frogs, toads, newts and salamanders are all amphibians. Characteristics of amphibians are: 1) They have spines; 2) They are cold-blooded; 3) They are hatched from eggs; 4) They have lungs, but they also breathe through their skin; 5) The skin of reptiles is smooth without hair, fur, feathers, or scales; 6) Reptiles must keep their skin wet, so they live in wet places; and 7) Although most have toes, they do not have claws. Many amphibians go through a change called **metamorphosis**. Frogs are born as fish-like tadpoles, breathing with gills. As they grow, they develop legs and lungs then lose the gills and tail. They spend their adult lives living on land.

Name the seven characteristics of amphibians.
1. _____
2. _____
3. _____
4. _____
5. _____
6. _____
7. _____

8. What word means "a change from one thing to another"?

   A. metamorphosis   B. amphibian   C. tadpole

Write **A** if the word is a characteristic of amphibians. Write **N** if it is not.

_____ 9. cold-blooded   _____ 10. scales   _____ 11. eggs
_____ 12. smooth skin   _____ 13. no claws   _____ 14. claws
_____ 15. live near water _____ 16. can fly   _____ 17. lungs
_____ 18. dry skin   _____ 19. has a spine   _____ 20. hair

Find it: Look online or in an encyclopedia to find the life cycle of a frog. Draw a chart and explain it to a friend or adult.

©2008 Plutarch Publications, Inc. PPI -1002

Name _____   Standard: Expository Comprehension

Insects

There are more insects on earth than any other class of animal. In fact, 95% of all animals are insects! They can live almost anywhere on Earth, including the ice caps at the north pole, but not many are found in the ocean. There are five main characteristics of insects: 1) Insects have three parts to their bodies including the head, thorax (chest) and abdomen (stomach); 2) They have six legs; 3) All insects have two pairs of wings and can fly; 4) Insects go through a metamorphosis and have four life stages. First they are eggs, then larva (like a worm), then they become a pupa (cocoon) and finally they are adults; and 5) Most adult insects have antennae or "feelers" on their head. They use the antennae to help them see, feel, smell and taste the world around them.

Name four of the five characteristics of insects.

1. _____
2. _____
3. _____
4. _____

Name four life stages in the metamorphosis of an insect.

5. _____
6. _____
7. _____
8. _____

Read the animal names. Write **S** if it is an insect and **N** if it is not.

_____ 9. robin   _____ 10. butterfly   _____ 11. squirrel
_____ 12. grasshopper _____ 13. worm   _____ 14. fly
_____ 15. cricket   _____ 16. beetle   _____ 17. duck
_____ 18. bat   _____ 19. mosquito   _____ 20. spider

Draw it: Find an insect and draw a picture of it. Label the head, thorax, and abdomen. Does it have antennae?

Name _____   Standard: Functional Comprehension

The Leaf

The cold winds blew.
Winter was on the way.
Most of the trees were bare,
But one leaf chose to stay.

It turned from green to red,
Got covered up with snow,
Stayed through the icy days.
But it wouldn't let go.

When days began to warm,
And birds began to sing,
The leaf was glad because
It had lasted until the spring!

1. What is the name of this poem?
   _____

2. In the first group of sentences, which season is coming?
   _____

3. In the first group of sentences, which word rhymes with "way"?
   _____

4. In the second group of sentences, what color did the leaf turn?
   _____

5. In the second group of sentences, which word rhymes with "go"?
   _____

6. In the third group of sentences, which season is coming?
   _____

7. In the third group of sentences, what was singing?
   _____

List the three changes in the weather the poem describes.
8. _____
9. _____
10. _____

11. At the end of the poem, why was the leaf happy?
    _____

Say it: Read the poem quietly to yourself. Now read it aloud to a friend or teacher.

Name _____ Standard: Functional Comprehension

Balloon

Green, yellow, red, blue
Any color just for you.
Fill with air, tie with string
It can do most anything.
As you walk it tags behind
Follows you, but will not mind.
Anywhere you want to go
Speedy fast or oh, so slow,
That balloon just floats around
Moves about without a sound.
Watch out... Stop!

POP

1. What is the name of this poem?
   _____

2. What colors are listed in the poem?
   _____

3. What does the balloon do when you walk?
   _____

4. What does the balloon sound like when it moves?
   _____

5. What is inside the balloon in this poem?
   _____

6. What does the line "As you walk it tags behind" mean?
   _____

7. Which words in the poem tell about the speed you move?
   _____

   List three pairs of rhyming words given in this poem.

8. _____
9. _____
10. _____

11. At the end of the poem, what happens to the balloon?
    _____

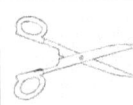 **Make it:** On a piece of paper, draw and color several balloons. Cut them out. Tape or glue them to a piece of construction paper. Add string to the bottom of each balloon.

Name _____ Standard: Functional Comprehension

Poem 1

Food
Tasty, hot
Cook, eat, enjoy
Good smells
Dinner

Poem 2

Bacon for breakfast
Eggs and pancakes on my plate
Syrup or jelly
And a glass of orange juice, too.
Breakfast, my favorite meal!

1. What is the main idea of Poem 1?
   _____

2. What is the main idea of Poem 2?
   _____

3. Do either of these poems rhyme?
   _____

4. Which poem do you like better? Why?
   _____
   _____
   _____
   _____

List three ways these two poems are alike.
6. _____
7. _____
8. _____

List three ways these two poems are different.
9. _____
10. _____
11. _____

Say it: Read the poem quietly to yourself. Now read it aloud to a friend or teacher.

©2008 Plutarch Publications, Inc. PPI-1002

Name _____   Standard: Functional Comprehension

heading
Sofia Davis
1122 Park Lane
Atco, NJ   08004

greeting Dear Sofia,

body
I can't believe it has already been four weeks since we left summer camp. It was fun sharing a cabin with you for those two weeks. I liked having you for a roommate. My favorite part was when we surprised Kate with that frog in her backpack. We sure had a good laugh! I hope we will see each other next summer, too. Please remember to write and tell me how school is going. I miss you!

closing Write back soon,
signature Nan Roberts

1. Who wrote this letter?
   _____

2. To whom was this letter written?
   _____

3. How do these two girls know each other?
   _____
   _____

4. Which word best describes these two girls?
   A. sisters   B. friends   C. cousins

5. Where does Sofia live?
   _____

6. For how long did these two girls share a cabin this summer?
   _____

Write about it: Write a short story that tells how Sofia and Nan put a frog in Kate's backpack.

©2008 Plutarch Publications, Inc. PPI -1002

Name _____   Standard: Functional Comprehension

heading → Chris Stone
884 Foxer Street
Clinton, TN   37716

greeting → Hi Chris,

body →   Can you come to my party next Saturday, March 5? I am taking a group of my friends to a dinosaur museum. We will see life-size models that move, just like the real dinosaurs. There is a sand pit where we can dig and find real dinosaur bones. There will be a movie that tells us how dinosaurs lived many years ago. We will even have dinosaur shaped french fries for lunch! I hope you can come.

closing → Your friend,
signature → Matt Bridges

1. Who wrote this letter?
   _____

2. To whom was this letter written?
   _____

3. What is Matt inviting Chris to do?
   _____
   _____

4. Where will the boys be able to find dinosaur bones?
      A. at the movie   B. at Matt's house   C. in a sand pit

5. In what city does Chris live?
   _____

6. What special treat will the boys be eating?
   _____

 **Draw it:** Draw a picture of the dinosaur you would like to see if you were invited to Matt's party.

Name _____   Standard: Functional Comprehension

heading
Abby McCall
1324 Lake Avenue
Boulder, CO 80303

greeting
Dear Abby,

body
 I would like to thank you for taking care of my plants and my dog, Earl, while I was away on vacation. I noticed that my rose bush bloomed just this morning and that is because you watered it every day. Earl is happy to have me home again, but he seems to miss you quite a bit. He looks out the window and whines, as if he is looking for you. Could you come over and play with him soon? He would like that!

closing
Sincerely,

signature
Mrs. Greene

1. Who wrote this letter?
   _____

2. To whom was this letter written?
   _____

3. What is the purpose of this letter?
   _____
   _____

4. How did Abby help the rose bush to bloom?
   A. she watered it   B. she weeded   C. she played with it

5. In what town does Abby live?
   _____

6. How does Mrs. Green know that Earl misses Abby?
   _____

Share it: Write a letter that thanks a friend for something. Share the letter with that friend.

©2008 Plutarch Publications, Inc. PPI -1002

Name _____   (Standard: Functional Comprehension)

DIRECTIONS: Read the clues given in each box. Decide what the clues are describing. Write your answer in the box.

I am alive. I have six legs. I am an animal. I am an insect. I have two sets of colorful wings. People enjoy watching me. I was once a caterpillar.	What am I?
I am nonliving. People buy me. I am made of paper. I tell many stories. I can be folded. People read me. I give you the news every day.	What am I?
I am nonliving. I have four legs. I have a back. I have two arms. I have a seat. I am found in homes and offices. Most people sit on me.	What am I?
I am alive. I am green. I have four legs. I live near water. I am a good swimmer. My back legs are very strong. I move by jumping.	What am I?
I am nonliving. I have windows. I have doors. I run. I am made of metal and glass. I take people places. I have four wheels.	What am I?

©2008 Plutarch Publications, Inc. PPI-1002

Name _____   Standard: Functional Comprehension

DIRECTIONS: Read the clues given in each box. Decide what the clues are describing. Write your answer in the box.

Clues	Answer
I am nonliving. I am round. I come in many colors. I am full of air. You use me to play games. I can be thrown or kicked. I like to bounce.	What am I?
I am living. I have a tail. I have four legs. I have fur. I am in the cat family. I roar and have sharp teeth. I have orange and black stripes.	What am I?
I have hands. I have a face. I move in circles. I am nonliving. You can read me. I sit on a table or hang on a wall. I tell you when it is time to do things.	What am I?
I have a round shape. I can keep you warm. I am bright. I help plants grow. You go around me every day. I am in the sky. You do not see me at night.	What am I?
I am nonliving. Most people enjoy me. I am written. I come in notes. You cannot see me. You listen to me. People use instruments to make me.	What am I?

Name _____   Standard: Functional Comprehension

DIRECTIONS: Read the clues given in each box. Decide what the clues are describing. Write your answer in the box.

I am nonliving. I am soft. I am in your house. I have four legs. You keep me covered up. You like me best when you are tired. You lay down on me.	What am I?
I am nonliving. I am round. I have two flat ends. I am useful. You can open me, but you can't close me again. I am made of metal. I keep food fresh.	What am I?
I am small. I am very hard. I am white. I have roots. I am used to cut and grind things. I am in your mouth. Most children have twenty-eight of me.	What am I?
No one likes me. You cannot see me. I can make you tired. I often visit in winter. Everyone gets me sooner or later. You don't feel well when I visit you. I make you sneeze and cough.	What am I?
I am nonliving. You cannot see me. You cannot taste me. I weigh nothing. I can be strong enough to push trees down. I can cool you on a hot day. You breathe me in and out.	What am I?

©2008 Plutarch Publications, Inc. PPI-1002

ANSWER KEYS: 6, 7, 8, 9

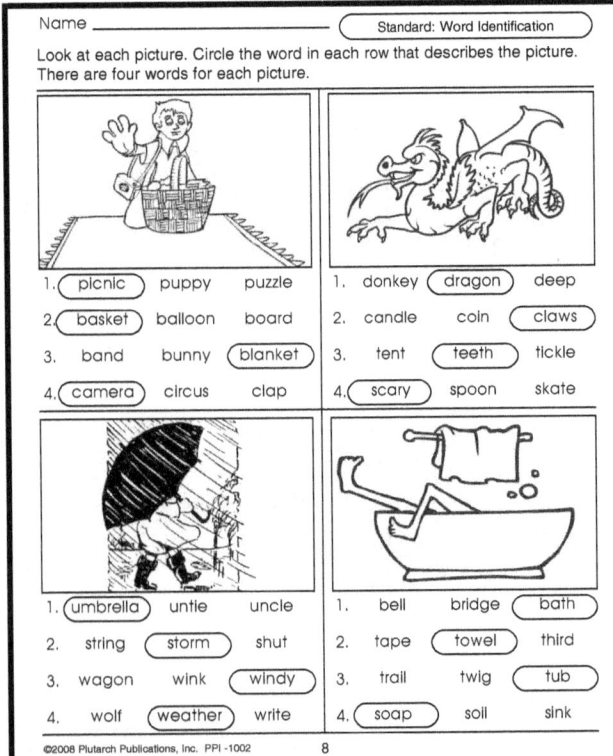

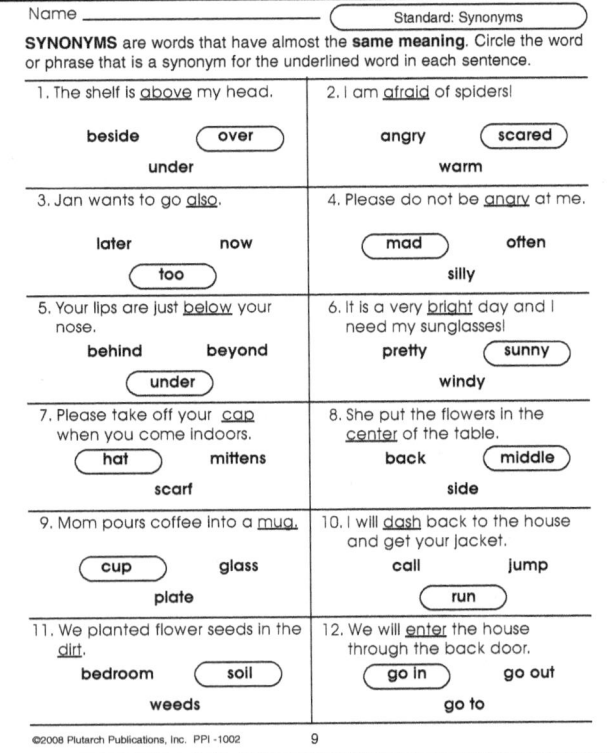

ANSWER KEYS: 10, 11, 12, 13

Page 10 — Standard: Synonyms

SYNONYMS are words that have almost the **same meaning**. Circle the word or phrase that is a synonym for the underlined word in each sentence.

1. Dad put <u>extra</u> cookies in my lunch.
   any — (**more**) — some

2. Judy was the <u>final</u> person in line.
   first — (**last**) — only

3. Put the paint away when you <u>finish</u>.
   begin — draw — (**end**)

4. That big dog <u>frightens</u> me!
   fights — growls — (**scares**)

5. Be sure to throw away your <u>garbage</u>.
   plate — (**trash**) — trunk

6. That was a <u>difficult</u> test!
   easy — (**hard**) — jolly

7. Many birds build nests in that <u>huge</u> tree.
   (**big**) — little — tiny

8. That <u>lady</u> is my neighbor.
   girl — lonely — (**woman**)

9. Can you <u>leap</u> over the fence?
   gallop — (**jump**) — walk

10. I went to the ocean <u>once</u> and saw a shark!
    fish — often — (**one time**)

11. Put the water in this <u>pail</u>.
    (**bucket**) — glass — hole

12. We can use <u>paste</u> to fix the tear in that paper.
    butter — (**glue**) — wax

Page 11 — Standard: Synonyms

SYNONYMS are words that have almost the **same meaning**. Circle the word or phrase that is a synonym for the underlined word in each sentence.

1. The gum costs one <u>penny</u>.
   (**cent**) — dime — dollar

2. Sue got three <u>presents</u> for her birthday.
   boxes — (**gifts**) — stripes

3. Joe did his work <u>quickly</u>!
   (**fast**) — slow — well

4. The man had to <u>repair</u> the flat tire on his car.
   bend — (**fix**) — slide

5. Do not be in a <u>rush</u> to grow up!
   busy — drop — (**hurry**)

6. We put the groceries in a brown paper <u>sack</u>.
   (**bag**) — truck — wagon

7. Please <u>shut</u> the door to keep the rain out.
   catch — (**close**) — slam

8. Mrs. Jones ate too much and now she feels <u>sick</u>.
   good — (**ill**) — tired

9. We need more <u>space</u> to hang this big mirror.
   clay — nails — (**room**)

10. Will you <u>toss</u> that ball to me?
    loose — roll — (**throw**)

11. This <u>trail</u> goes right through the forest.
    (**path**) — tree — travel

12. The bird used <u>twigs</u> to build a nest.
    feathers — newspapers — (**sticks**)

Page 12 — Standard: Antonyms

ANTONYMS are words that have **opposite meanings**. Circle the word or phrase that is an antonym for the underlined word in each sentence.

1. Put this picture <u>above</u> the other on the wall.
   (**below**) — over — next to

2. Josh was <u>behind</u> you in line.
   (**ahead of**) — after — next to

3. Those sisters are <u>alike</u> in many ways.
   almost — (**different**) — the same

4. Jen was <u>angry</u> that she missed the party.
   (**happy**) — mad — upset

5. Those children are hard to keep <u>apart</u>.
   away — awake — (**together**)

6. The baby is <u>asleep</u> now.
   (**awake**) — eating — napping

7. Do your work <u>before</u> dinner.
   (**after**) — beside — with

8. Tape the <u>bottom</u> of the box.
   below — side — (**top**)

9. Would you like to <u>sell</u> those pencils?
   (**buy**) — take — use

10. The weather seems a little <u>cool</u> today.
    cold — snowy — (**warm**)

11. My bedroom is <u>downstairs</u>.
    clean — indoors — (**upstairs**)

12. The dishes are not <u>dry</u> yet.
    done — (**wet**) — wild

Page 13 — Standard: Antonyms

ANTONYMS are words that have **opposite meanings**. Circle the word or phrase that is an antonym for the underlined word in each sentence.

1. Daddy came home <u>early</u> from work.
   before — (**late**) — whenever

2. It is <u>easy</u> to draw a flower.
   fast — fun — (**hard**)

3. The bucket is <u>empty</u>.
   (**full**) — lonely — warm

4. <u>Everybody</u> loved the school play!
   All of us — (**Nobody**) — They

5. Peter drew a <u>thin</u> line across the board.
   bare — careful — (**wide**)

6. There are <u>few</u> people who want to help.
   busy — less — (**many**)

7. I have the <u>final</u> piece of the puzzle!
   (**first**) — last — shape

8. It is time to <u>finish</u> your lunch.
   own — (**start**) — stop

9. I <u>forgot</u> where I put my book.
   almost — belong — (**remembered**)

10. Judy <u>loves</u> to watch scary movies.
    favorite — (**hates**) — likes

11. Kyle's mother made a <u>huge</u> pie for us to share.
    big — large — (**tiny**)

12. Be <u>quiet</u>. The baby is sleeping.
    careful — (**loud**) — proud

ANSWER KEYS: 14, 15, 16, 17

Name _____ Standard: Antonyms

ANTONYMS are words that have **opposite meanings**. Circle the word or phrase that is an antonym for the underlined word in each sentence.

1. We must play <u>indoors</u> today.
   inside   (outside)   together

2. That <u>poor</u> family lives in the old house at the end of the street.
   nice   office   (rich)

3. Father will <u>repair</u> the flat tire on my bike.
   (break)   fix   sell

4. Your hand feels <u>rough</u> and dry.
   hard   sharp   (smooth)

5. Please <u>shut</u> the door for me.
   close   find   (open)

6. My pillow is <u>softer</u> than my blanket.
   better   (harder)   nicer

7. The map shows that we need to go <u>south</u> on Elm Street.
   east   home   (north)

8. Darla has <u>straight</u> hair.
   (curly)   fine   thin

9. The weather is <u>terrible</u> today!
   awful   bad   (wonderful)

10. My shoes are too <u>tight</u> and don't fit well.
    fresh   (loose)   old

11. That <u>ugly</u> dog does great tricks!
    mean   (pretty)   young

12. We must <u>whisper</u> in class.
    talk   whistle   (yell)

Name _____ Standard: Spelling

One word in each group below is not spelled correctly. Put an **X** in the box next to the word that is NOT correct.

- ☐ yell
- ☐ backyard
- ☐ twig
- ☐ frighten
- ☒ fense
- ☒ stik
- ☐ scary
- ☐ swing
- ☐ tree
- ☒ afrad
- ☐ play
- ☐ forest

- ☐ bird
- ☐ Monday
- ☐ nine
- ☐ robin
- ☐ Tuesday
- ☒ sevn
- ☒ nesst
- ☒ Wedesday
- ☐ three
- ☐ flew
- ☐ Thursday
- ☐ six

- ☒ yaer
- ☐ spring
- ☒ sangwich
- ☐ month
- ☒ sumer
- ☐ milk
- ☐ day
- ☐ fall
- ☐ lunch
- ☐ week
- ☐ winter
- ☐ cookie

- ☐ wolf
- ☒ musick
- ☐ happy
- ☐ growl
- ☐ band
- ☐ hope
- ☒ teth
- ☐ piano
- ☐ felt
- ☐ pack
- ☐ lesson
- ☒ carefull

Name _____ Standard: Spelling

One word in each group below is not spelled correctly. Put an **X** in the box next to the word that is NOT correct.

- ☐ the
- ☐ monster
- ☒ beddroom
- ☐ there
- ☐ ugly
- ☐ lamp
- ☒ thier
- ☒ screem
- ☐ blanket
- ☐ they're
- ☐ scare
- ☐ quilt

- ☐ evening
- ☐ swing
- ☐ boot
- ☐ moonlight
- ☒ brige
- ☒ mudd
- ☐ wind
- ☐ park
- ☐ rain
- ☒ breze
- ☐ pond
- ☐ storm

- ☐ family
- ☒ donkie
- ☐ horse
- ☐ dress
- ☐ barn
- ☒ babby
- ☐ aunt
- ☐ quack
- ☐ raccoon
- ☒ wooman
- ☐ mice
- ☐ worm

- ☒ nobbody
- ☐ basement
- ☒ befor
- ☐ everybody
- ☐ roof
- ☐ after
- ☐ anybody
- ☒ hous
- ☐ soon
- ☐ anyone
- ☐ yard
- ☐ never

Name _____ Standard: Spelling

One word in each group below is not spelled correctly. Put an **X** in the box next to the word that is NOT correct.

- ☐ beach
- ☐ mountain
- ☐ write
- ☐ sand
- ☒ clim
- ☐ spell
- ☒ shor
- ☐ bush
- ☐ count
- ☐ swim
- ☐ trip
- ☒ reade

- ☒ fealings
- ☐ crayon
- ☐ two
- ☐ brave
- ☐ pencil
- ☐ four
- ☐ unhappy
- ☐ pen
- ☐ five
- ☐ upset
- ☒ papper
- ☒ eght

- ☐ garden
- ☐ north
- ☐ ship
- ☐ farm
- ☒ soth
- ☐ ocean
- ☒ chiken
- ☐ east
- ☒ floot
- ☐ ranch
- ☐ west
- ☐ captain

- ☒ clok
- ☐ morning
- ☐ dish
- ☐ time
- ☒ afternon
- ☐ plate
- ☐ minute
- ☐ evening
- ☐ spoon
- ☐ hour
- ☐ night
- ☒ dinnar

ANSWER KEYS: 18, 19, 20, 21

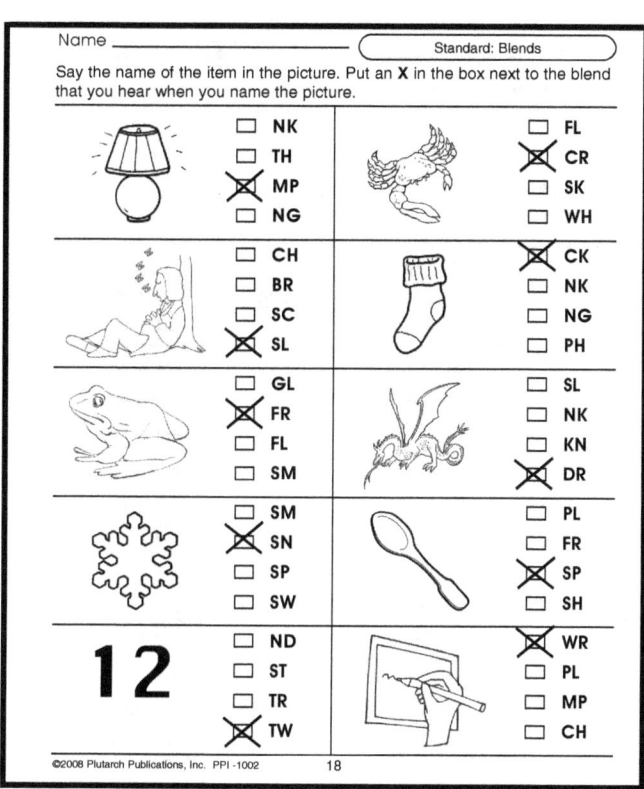
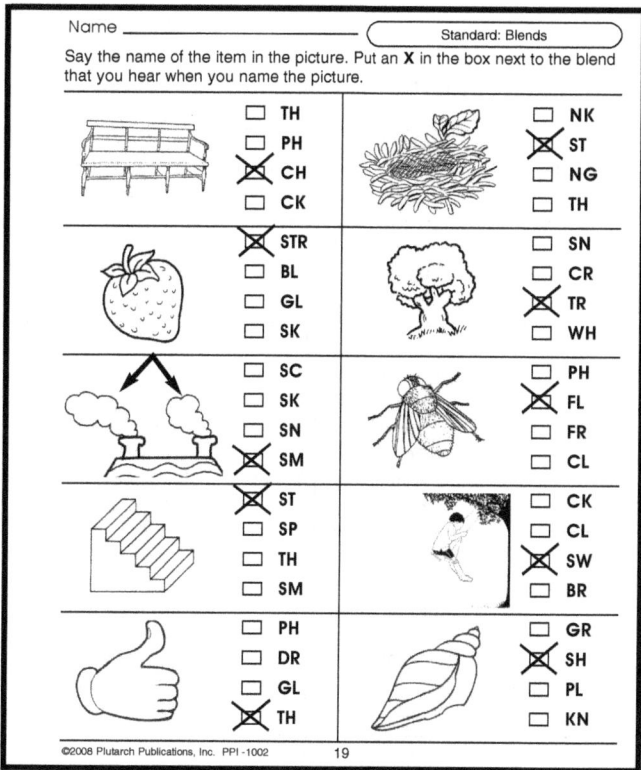
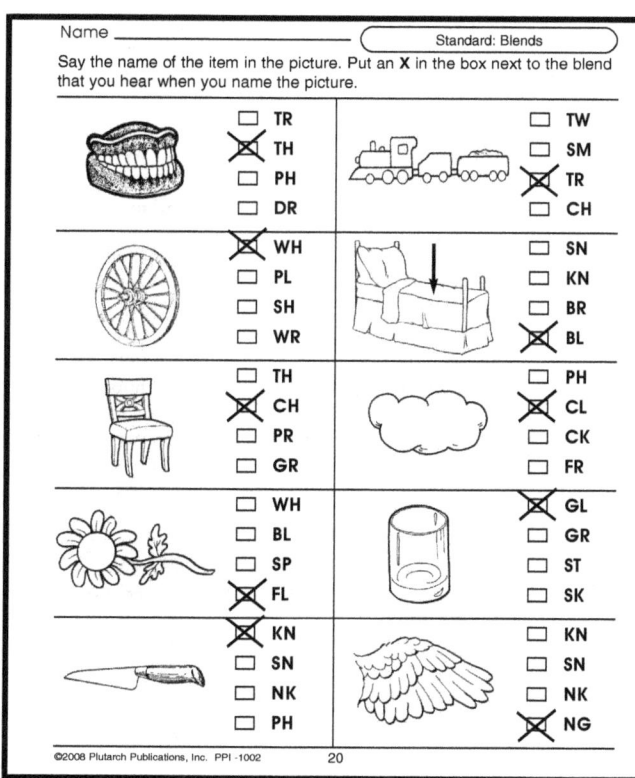
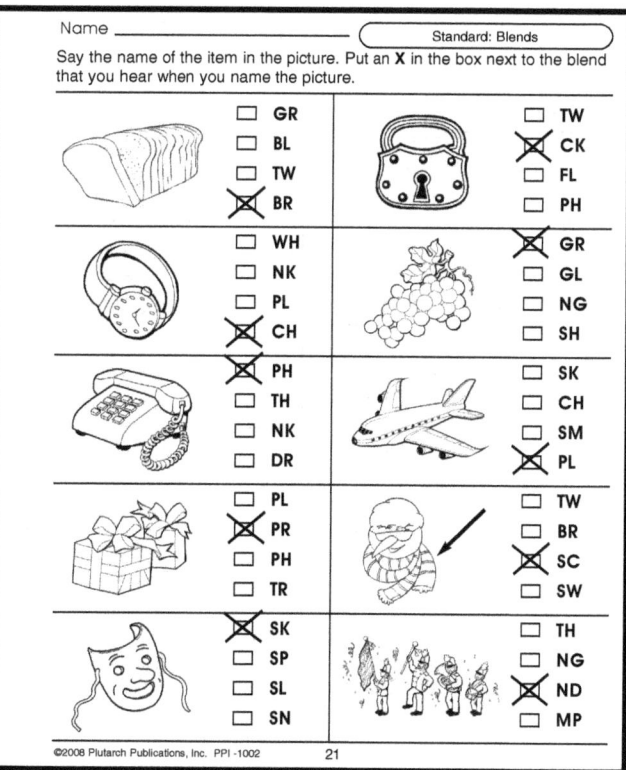

ANSWER KEYS: 22, 23, 24, 25

Name _____ Standard: Vowels

Read each word and listen to the sound of the letters that are underlined. Put and **X** in the box next to the word that has the same sound as the underlined letters.

1. gr<u>ow</u>	☐ cow ☒ coat ☐ flood	2. br<u>a</u>ce	☐ carry ☐ gather ☒ lady
3. m<u>u</u>sic	☒ rule ☐ upset ☐ touch	4. l<u>i</u>ck	☐ size ☐ sight ☒ silly
5. m<u>u</u>d	☐ true ☒ summer ☐ fruit	6. <u>a</u>gree	☐ able ☒ idea ☐ lean
7. m<u>oa</u>n	☒ own ☐ won ☐ prove	8. ch<u>ie</u>f	☐ blew ☐ neck ☒ either
9. y<u>a</u>rd	☐ wake ☐ raise ☒ farm	10. w<u>i</u>tch	☐ quiet ☒ quilt ☐ nine
11. f<u>oo</u>d	☒ moon ☐ trot ☐ join	12. m<u>ou</u>th	☐ some ☐ low ☒ south

---

Name _____ Standard: Vowels

Read each word and listen to the sound of the letters that are underlined. Put and **X** in the box next to the word that has the same sound as the underlined letters.

1. tr<u>u</u>th	☐ funny ☒ flute ☐ aunt	2. p<u>o</u>ny	☒ rose ☐ month ☐ done
3. c<u>a</u>ge	☐ nap ☐ smart ☒ plate	4. str<u>aw</u>	☐ sail ☐ strange ☒ draw
5. br<u>o</u>ke	☒ blow ☐ done ☐ loud	6. qu<u>i</u>ck	☒ string ☐ tight ☐ piece
7. tr<u>u</u>nk	☐ burn ☒ pump ☐ four	8. fr<u>ee</u>	☐ held ☐ earth ☒ meat
9. t<u>igh</u>ten	☒ pipe ☐ visit ☐ milk	10. cr<u>a</u>b	☐ share ☒ trap ☐ warm
11. sp<u>oo</u>n	☐ good ☐ indoor ☒ tool	12. b<u>u</u>rn	☐ stair ☒ fur ☐ drum

---

Name _____ Standard: Vowels

Read each word and listen to the sound of the letters that are underlined. Put and **X** in the box next to the word that has the same sound as the underlined letters.

1. kn<u>i</u>fe	☐ flip ☐ dirt ☒ fight	2. sh<u>a</u>rp	☐ clay ☐ chair ☒ smart
3. l<u>oo</u>se	☐ look ☒ school ☐ foot	4. cl<u>ow</u>n	☐ low ☐ lock ☒ town
5. l<u>u</u>nch	☐ music ☒ dug ☐ blue	6. c<u>oi</u>n	☒ joy ☐ cool ☐ monkey
7. cl<u>ue</u>	☐ hunt ☒ June ☐ dust	8. d<u>i</u>rt	☐ bright ☐ drive ☒ bird
9. pl<u>a</u>nt	☒ band ☐ bake ☐ hair	10. d<u>i</u>sh	☒ prince ☐ ice ☐ five
11. h<u>u</u>ng	☐ Tuesday ☐ yourself ☒ rush	12. l<u>o</u>ck	☐ snow ☒ shot ☐ pool

---

Name _____ Standard: Vowels

Read each word and listen to the sound of the letters that are underlined. Put and **X** in the box next to the word that has the same sound as the underlined letters.

1. sk<u>a</u>te	☐ machine ☒ taste ☐ candy	2. thr<u>ew</u>	☐ weed ☐ scream ☒ root
3. dr<u>u</u>m	☒ hunt ☐ moon ☐ hour	4. d<u>e</u>sk	☐ sheet ☐ teach ☒ net
5. l<u>ie</u>	☒ sigh ☐ pink ☐ met	6. sh<u>ow</u>	☐ now ☒ hope ☐ done
7. h<u>u</u>nt	☒ thumb ☐ four ☐ huge	8. sm<u>a</u>rt	☐ pair ☐ salt ☒ yard
9. sh<u>o</u>rt	☐ moan ☒ porch ☐ patch	10. c<u>au</u>ght	☒ walk ☐ enough ☐ warm
11. ind<u>ee</u>d	☒ beat ☐ belt ☐ feather	12. bl<u>a</u>nket	☐ mark ☐ grade ☒ cap

ANSWER KEYS: 26, 27, 28, 29

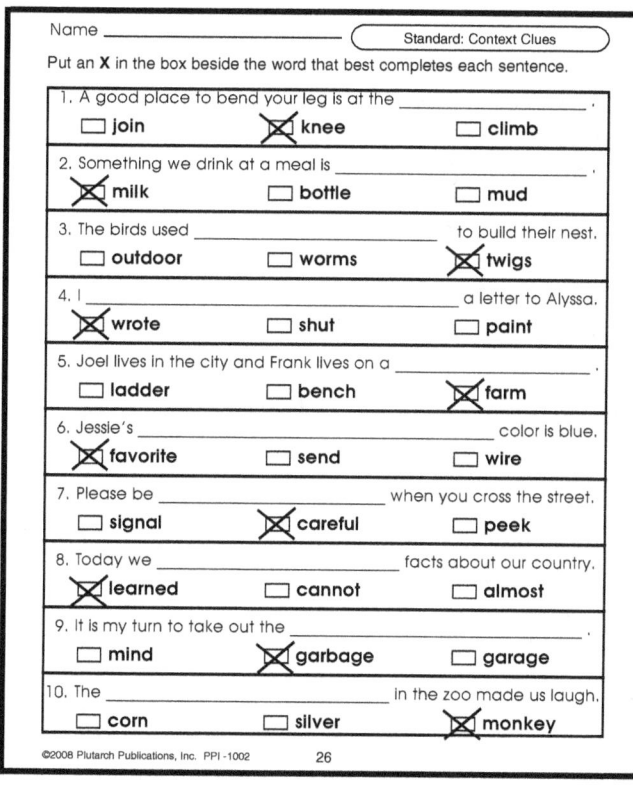

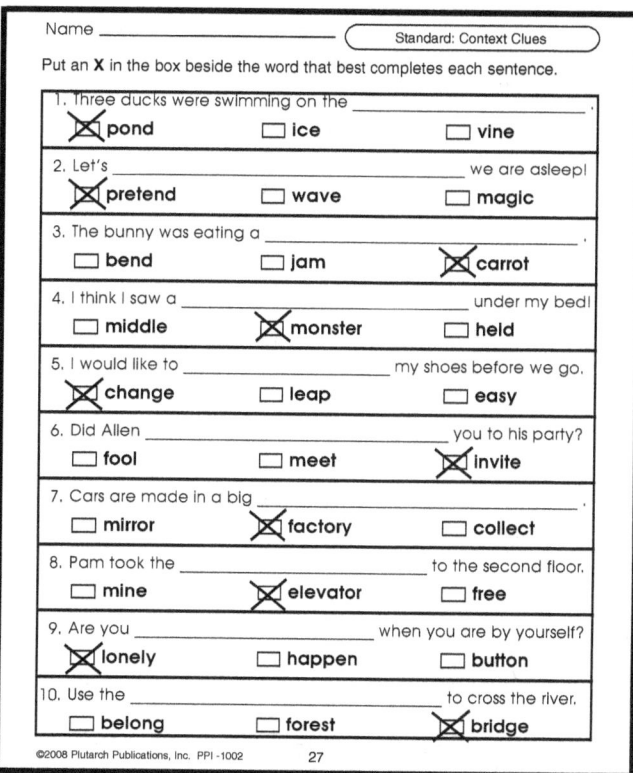

ANSWER KEYS: 30, 31, 32, 33

Name _____ Standard: Sequence of Events

Sequence means to put things in order. For each group below, number the items in the order given.

Youngest to Oldest:
- 3 child
- 6 grandparent
- 4 teenager
- 1 baby
- 2 toddler
- 5 parent

Small to Large:
- 5 beachball
- 3 baseball
- 1 pea
- 2 golf ball
- 4 basketball
- 6 planet

Light to Heavy:
- 6 elephant
- 1 snail
- 3 rabbit
- 2 frog
- 5 horse
- 4 dog

Least to Most:
- 3 dime
- 1 penny
- 4 quarter
- 6 dollar
- 2 nickel
- 5 half dollar

Shortest to Longest:
- 5 month
- 3 day
- 4 week
- 1 minute
- 6 year
- 2 hour

A to Z:
- 5 strawberry
- 4 peach
- 1 apple
- 3 grapes
- 2 banana
- 6 watermelon

Name _____ Standard: Sequence of Events

Sequence of Events is the order in which things happen. Below are things we see or do each day. Number them in order from first to last, just as they should happen.

My Day:
- 3 I eat my breakfast.
- 5 I work and play at school.
- 1 I wake up.
- 6 The bus brings me home.
- 7 I eat my dinner.
- 2 I get out of bed.
- 4 The bus takes me to school.
- 8 I go to bed.

Make a Cake:
- 1 Buy a cake mix.
- 6 Pour the batter into a pan.
- 8 Bake until it is finished.
- 4 Add eggs and milk to the mix.
- 2 Get out the bowl and spoon.
- 5 Stir until it's well mixed.
- 3 Put the mix in the bowl.
- 7 Put the pan in the oven.

Buying Gum:
- 7 Pick up your package.
- 6 Get your change back.
- 3 Choose the gum you like.
- 2 Look at all the gum.
- 1 Go to the store.
- 8 Leave the store.
- 5 Pay the cashier.
- 4 Get in line to check out.

Wash Your Face:
- 2 Wet the washcloth.
- 4 Wash your face.
- 6 Rinse your face.
- 7 Dry your face.
- 5 Rinse soap off the washcloth.
- 3 Put soap on the washcloth.
- 1 Turn on the water.
- 8 Turn off the water.

Name _____ Standard: Sequence of Events

Read the story.

Randy's Garden

Randy wanted a garden in his backyard. First he dug up the grass. Next he hoed the dirt until it was loose. Then he planted a row of carrot seeds. After that he planted a row of lettuce seeds. Finally he planted a row of tomato seedlings. What a good garden!

Read these sentences.

He planted carrots in the first row.
The last things planted were tomato seedlings.
Randy used a hoe to loosen the dirt.
Randy dug up the grass.
Next, lettuce seeds were planted.

On the lines below, write the sentences in order as they happened in the story.

1. **RANDY DUG UP THE GRASS.**
2. **RANDY USED THE HOE TO LOOSEN THE DIRT.**
3. **HE PLANTED CARROTS IN THE FIRST ROW.**
4. **NEXT, LETTUCE SEEDS WERE PLANTED.**
5. **THE LAST THINGS PLANTED WERE TOMATO SEEDLINGS.**

Name _____ Standard: Fact or Opinion

A **FACT** is something that is real and can be proven.
An **OPINION** is a belief or the way you feel about something.

Read the statements below. Decide if each is a fact or an opinion. On the blank, write **F** if it is fact and **O** if it is opinion.

- F 1. There are twenty-four hours in every day.
- O 2. We should use more hours for playing than for working.
- F 3. Each day has a morning, afternoon, evening, and night.
- O 4. Afternoons are more fun than mornings.
- O 5. Six o'clock is the very best time to eat dinner.
- F 6. The sun rises in the morning and sets in the evening.
- F 7. Stars can be seen in the night sky.
- O 8. The moon is beautiful to look at.
- F 9. There are seven days in a week.
- O 10. One week is a long time.
- O 11. Monday is the worst day of the week.
- O 12. Saturday is the best day of the week.
- O 13. Wednesday is a hard word to spell!
- F 14. Thursday is the day before Friday.
- O 15. Sunday is always a good day for a picnic.
- F 16. Tuesday is the day before Wednesday.
- O 17. A week of summer is more fun than a week of winter.
- F 18. There are 30 or 31 days in every month except February.
- F 19. There are twelve months in a year.
- O 20. October is the best month because it has Halloween!

Write one fact and one opinion about any month you choose.

Fact: **MY BIRTHDAY IS IN OCTOBER.**
(ANSWERS MAY VARY)
Opinion: **OCTOBER IS THE BEST MONTH OF THE YEAR!**

ANSWER KEYS: 34, 35, 36, 37

Name _____ Standard: Fact or Opinion

A **FACT** is something that is real and can be proven.
An **OPINION** is a belief or the way you feel about something.

Read the statements below. Decide if each is a fact or an opinion.
On the blank, write **F** if it is fact and **O** if it is opinion.

- _F_ 1. Fruit comes from plants.
- _O_ 2. Oranges and lemons are the best kind of fruit.
- _O_ 3. Lemons are prettier because they are yellow.
- _F_ 4. Oranges and lemons grow on trees.
- _O_ 5. The flowers on the orange tree smell better than roses!
- _F_ 6. Strawberries and blueberries are fruit.
- _F_ 7. Strawberries are red.
- _O_ 8. Blueberries taste best in a pie.
- _O_ 9. Strawberry jam is better than blueberry jam.
- _F_ 10. Grapes can be red or green.
- _O_ 11. Red grapes are better than green grapes.
- _F_ 12. Grapes grow in bunches.
- _F_ 13. Grapes are dried to make raisins.
- _O_ 14. Apples are the best fruit of all!
- _F_ 15. Apples can be red, green, or yellow.
- _O_ 16. Apple pie is better than blueberry or lemon pie.
- _F_ 17. Apples grow on trees.
- _F_ 18. Fruit is a healthy food to eat.
- _O_ 19. The best snacks are made with fruit.
- _O_ 20. All fruit tastes great!

Write one fact and one opinion about any fruit you choose.
Fact: __PLUMS ARE PURPLE OR RED.__
_____(ANSWERS MAY VARY)
Opinion: __PLUMS ARE BEST WHEN THEY ARE COLD!__

©2008 Plutarch Publications, Inc. PPI-1002   34

Name _____ Standard: Fact or Opinion

A **FACT** is something that is real and can be proven.
An **OPINION** is a belief or the way you feel about something.

Read the statements below. Decide if each is a fact or an opinion.
On the blank, write **F** if it is fact and **O** if it is opinion.

- _F_ 1. Dogs, cats, birds, and rabbits are common pets.
- _O_ 2. Large black dogs are the nicest pets.
- _F_ 3. Many people own dogs.
- _O_ 4. Small dogs are best because they can live indoors.
- _F_ 5. Dogs can bark and wag their tails.
- _F_ 6. Some dogs have long fur.
- _O_ 7. Girls think cats are better than dogs.
- _F_ 8. Cats meow.
- _O_ 9. Cats are sneaky and mean.
- _O_ 10. All cats are mean to dogs and mice.
- _F_ 11. Pet birds often live in cages.
- _O_ 12. Birds are noisy and not nice pets.
- _F_ 13. Some people have parrots as pets.
- _O_ 14. Birds are beautiful and fun to watch.
- _O_ 15. Rabbits are the cutest pets because they have long ears!
- _F_ 16. Rabbits hop and eat lettuce.
- _O_ 17. Rabbits do not make good pets.
- _O_ 18. Birds are nicer than rabbits and cats.
- _O_ 19. The best pets of all are fish.
- _O_ 20. Dogs, cats, birds, and rabbits make the best pets.

Write one fact and one opinion about a pet you choose.
Fact: __BIRDS HAVE FEATHERS.__
_____(ANSWERS MAY VARY)
Opinion: __MICE MAKE THE BEST PETS OF ALL!__

©2008 Plutarch Publications, Inc. PPI-1002   35

Name _____ Standard: Compare/Contrast

We **compare** and **contrast** things to find out
how they are **alike** and how they are **different**.

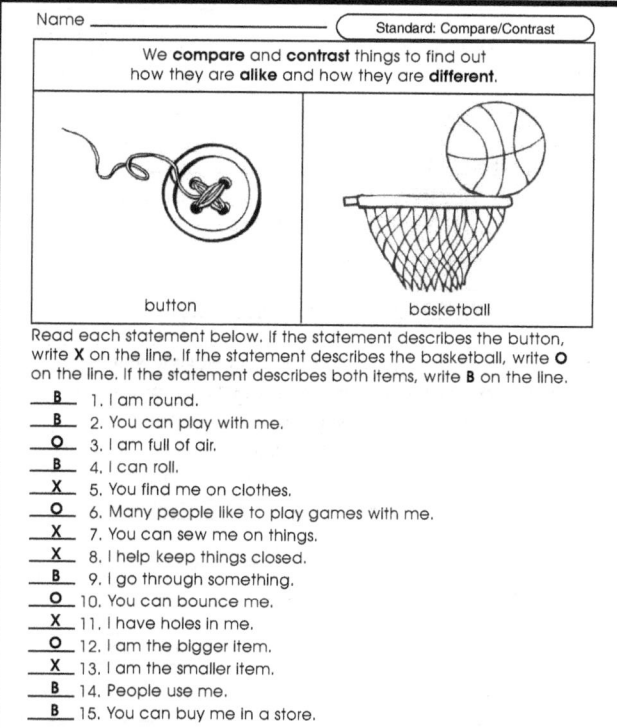

button | basketball

Read each statement below. If the statement describes the button,
write **X** on the line. If the statement describes the basketball, write **O**
on the line. If the statement describes both items, write **B** on the line.

- _B_ 1. I am round.
- _B_ 2. You can play with me.
- _O_ 3. I am full of air.
- _B_ 4. I can roll.
- _X_ 5. You find me on clothes.
- _O_ 6. Many people like to play games with me.
- _X_ 7. You can sew on things.
- _X_ 8. I help keep things closed.
- _B_ 9. I go through something.
- _O_ 10. You can bounce me.
- _X_ 11. I have holes in me.
- _O_ 12. I am the bigger item.
- _X_ 13. I am the smaller item.
- _B_ 14. People use me.
- _B_ 15. You can buy me in a store.

©2008 Plutarch Publications, Inc. PPI-1002   36

Name _____ Standard: Compare/Contrast

We **compare** and **contrast** things to find out
how they are **alike** and how they are **different**.

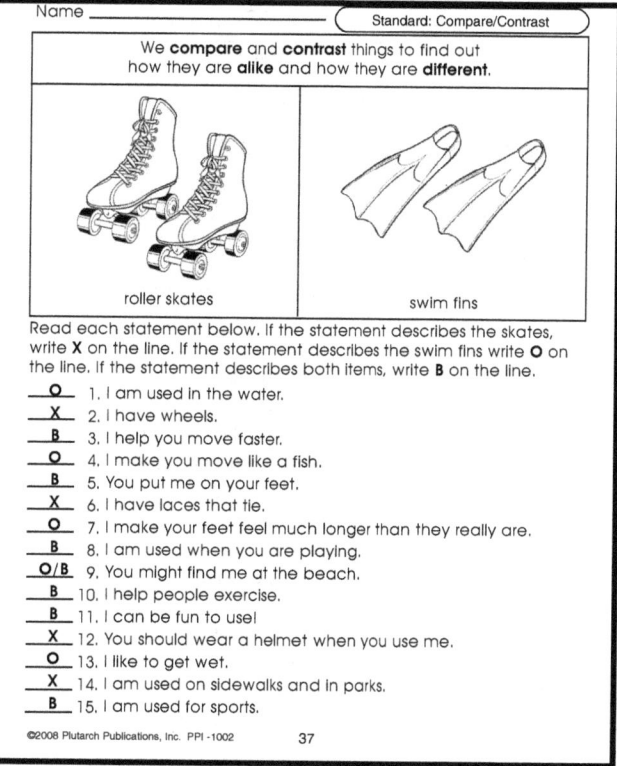

roller skates | swim fins

Read each statement below. If the statement describes the skates,
write **X** on the line. If the statement describes the swim fins write **O** on
the line. If the statement describes both items, write **B** on the line.

- _O_ 1. I am used in the water.
- _X_ 2. I have wheels.
- _B_ 3. I help you move faster.
- _O_ 4. I make you move like a fish.
- _B_ 5. You put me on your feet.
- _X_ 6. I have laces that tie.
- _O_ 7. I make your feet feel much longer than they really are.
- _B_ 8. I am used when you are playing.
- _O/B_ 9. You might find me at the beach.
- _B_ 10. I help people exercise.
- _B_ 11. I can be fun to use!
- _X_ 12. You should wear a helmet when you use me.
- _O_ 13. I like to get wet.
- _X_ 14. I am used on sidewalks and in parks.
- _B_ 15. I am used for sports.

©2008 Plutarch Publications, Inc. PPI-1002   37

ANSWER KEYS: 38, 39, 40, 41

Name _____ Standard: Compare/Contrast

We **compare** and **contrast** things to find out how they are **alike** and how they are **different**.

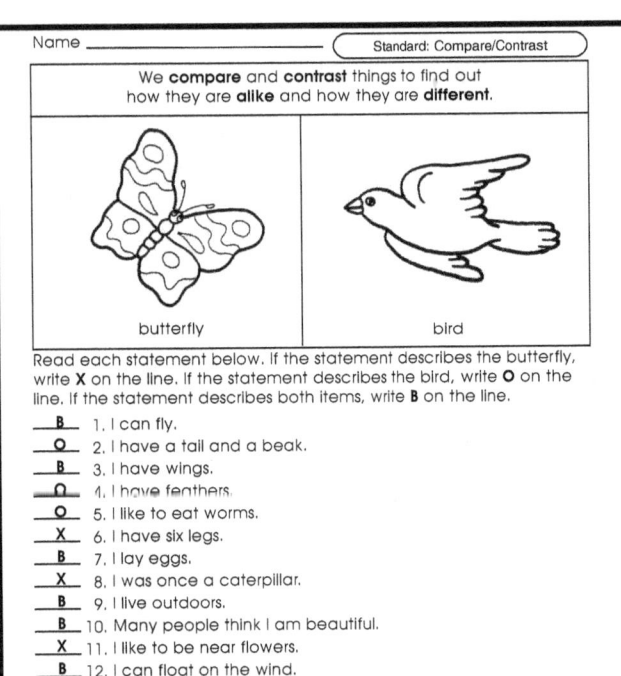

| butterfly | bird |

Read each statement below. If the statement describes the butterfly, write **X** on the line. If the statement describes the bird, write **O** on the line. If the statement describes both items, write **B** on the line.

- **B** 1. I can fly.
- **O** 2. I have a tail and a beak.
- **B** 3. I have wings.
- **O** 4. I have feathers.
- **O** 5. I like to eat worms.
- **X** 6. I have six legs.
- **B** 7. I lay eggs.
- **X** 8. I was once a caterpillar.
- **B** 9. I live outdoors.
- **B** 10. Many people think I am beautiful.
- **X** 11. I like to be near flowers.
- **B** 12. I can float on the wind.
- **O** 13. I make a sound like a whistle.
- **X** 14. I make no sound at all.
- **O** 15. I live in a nest.

Name _____ Standard: Story Elements

Story Elements:
Title: the name of the book
Author: the person who wrote the story
Illustrator: the person who drew the pictures for the book
Characters: the people or things about whom the story is told
Plot: the events that happen in the story
Setting: when and where the story takes place

Read the statements below. On the line write **T** if the statement is about the title, **A** for author, **I** for illustrator, **C** for characters, **P** for plot, or **S** for setting.

- **T** 1. *James and the Giant Peach* is a very good book.
- **C** 2. This story is about a boy named James Henry Trotter.
- **I** 3. The pictures by Nancy Ekholm Burkert are beautiful!
- **S** 4. The story takes place in England and New York.
- **P** 5. James lives with his two mean aunts who do not like him.
- **A** 6. Roald Dahl wrote this story.
- **P** 7. A spilled bag of magic green things makes a giant peach grow on the old peach tree during the night.
- **P** 8. James has many adventures with a group of giant insects.
- **C** 9. Ladybug is very kind to James.
- **C** 10. Grasshopper plays music with his wings and legs.
- **P** 11. The peach rolls to the ocean and sharks try to eat it.
- **P** 12. Birds fly the peach to New York.
- **C** 13. Centipede tells silly stories and is funny.
- **P** 14. The peach lands on the Empire State Building.
- **P** 15. Henry and his friends end up living in New York.

Name _____ Standard: Story Elements

Story Elements:
Title: the name of the book
Author: the person who wrote the story
Illustrator: the person who drew the pictures for the book
Characters: the people or things about whom the story is told
Plot: the events that happen in the story
Setting: when and where the story takes place

Read the statements below. On the line write **T** if the statement is about the title, **A** for author, **I** for illustrator, **C** for characters, **P** for plot, or **S** for setting.

- **T** 1. A good book to read is *The Very Quiet Cricket*.
- **C** 2. The story is about a young cricket.
- **S** 3. The story takes place in a field.
- **P** 4. The cricket does not know how to make noise with his wings.
- **P** 5. Different insects say hello, but the cricket cannot answer.
- **I** 6. The pictures by Eric Carle are painted on glass.
- **P** 7. The little cricket keeps rubbing his wings together, but he cannot make a sound.
- **C** 8. A locust and dragonfly are two of the animals in the book.
- **C** 9. The bumblebee buzzes.
- **C/P** 10. A beautiful luna moth flys by at night.
- **C/P** 11. The cricket is sad because he cannot chirp.
- **P** 12. The cricket meets another quiet little cricket.
- **P** 13. The very quiet cricket rubs his wings once more and chirps!
- **P** 14. The chirp is the most beautiful sound they have ever heard.
- **A** 15. Eric Carle wrote this and many other books.

Name _____ Standard: Story Elements

A book report tells about all the story elements. Choose your favorite book and use this book report to tell about it. **(ANSWERS MAY VARY)**

Title of the book: **BLUEBERRIES FOR SAL**

Author: **ROBERT McCLOSKEY**
Illustrator: **ROBERT McCLOSKEY**
Characters: **SAL, MOTHER, BEAR, BABY BEAR**

Setting: **A SUMMER DAY ON A HILL IN MAINE**

Plot: **(SCORE 3 PTS TOTAL) SAL GOES BLUEBERRY PICKING WITH HER MOTHER ONE WARM SUMMER DAY. SAL EATS MOST OF HER BERRIES AND GETS TIRED SO SHE WANDERS AWAY FROM MOTHER. ON THE OTHER SIDE OF THE HILL, BABY BEAR AND HIS MOTHER ARE DOING THE SAME THINGS. SAL RUNS INTO MOTHER BEAR WHILE BABY BEAR RUNS INTO MOTHER. THE MOTHERS QUICKLY FIND THEIR OWN CHILDREN AND LEAVE THE HILL.**

Things I liked about the book: **SAL IS LIKE ME. I LIKED THE SOUND AS SAL DROPPED THE BLUEBERRIES INTO THE PAIL.**

Things I didn't like about the book: **MOTHER BEAR WAS SCARY!**

ANSWER KEYS: 42, 43, 44, 45

Name _____   Standard: Genre

Genre is the style in which a story is written. Two types of genre are:
  Fiction - a story that has been made up and didn't really happen
  Nonfiction - a story about people or events that are real

Read the statements below. On the line write **F** if the book is fiction (made up). Write **N** if the book is nonfiction (about a real person or event).

__F__ 1. *Amelia Bedelia Goes Camping*, by Peggy Parish, is a story about silly Amelia who mixes up the meaning of words. When she is told to pitch a tent, she throws it into a bush!

__N__ 2. Learn about the tracks that different animals leave in the mud and snow in *Animal Tracks*, a book by Arthur Dorros.

__N__ 3. *Nine True Dolphin Stories* by Margaret Davidson. This book gives facts about dolphins and their human friends.

__F__ 4. In the book *Danny and the Dinosaur* by Syd Hoff, a boy goes to a museum where a friendly dinosaur comes to life and they play together.

__F__ 5. Learn what it means to be true friends in the book *Frog and Toad are Friends* by Arnold Lobel. Toad helps Frog feel better when he is sick. Frog writes a letter to Toad when Toad is sad because he has no mail.

__N__ 6. *Skeletons! Skeletons!* by Katy Hall tells about the bones in our bodies.

__N__ 7. Find out how milk is made and how it gets to the store in the book *Milk Makers* by Gail Gibbons.

__F__ 8. *Morris Goes to School* by B. Wiseman, is a story about a moose who goes to school to learn to read and count.

©2008 Plutarch Publications, Inc. PPI-1002   42

Name _____   Standard: Narrative Comprehension

Juan likes to ride his bike. He rides it to school. He rides it to the store. He rides it around town! Juan is very fast on his bike. One day Juan was taking a ride with his friend, Pedro. They decided to have a race to see who was the faster rider. The race would begin at Pedro's driveway and end at the fence near the end of the block. The boys lined up their bikes. Ready, set, go! The boys sped down the sidewalk, each pushing hard on the pedals. Suddenly Juan saw a turtle crawling in his path. He slammed on the brakes and **skidded** to a stop. Pedro kept going and finally stopped at the fence. He turned around and rode back to Juan. Pedro declared that Juan was the winner, even though he did not finish the race. The two friends picked up the turtle and took it to the nearby creek where it would be safe from speeding bikes.

1. What are the names of the boys? __JUAN AND PEDRO__
2. Where did the race begin? __AT PEDRO'S DRIVEWAY__

Name three places Juan likes to ride his bike.
3. __TO SCHOOL__
4. __TO THE STORE__   (ANSWERS MAY VARY)
5. __AROUND TOWN__
6. Why did Juan stop during the race?
__A TURTLE CRAWLED INTO THE PATH OF HIS BIKE__

7. What word means almost the same as the word "skidded"?
   A. behind   (**B. slid**)   C. kicked
8. What would be a good title for this story?
   A. A Boy Named Pedro
   (**B. Juan and Pedro Race**)
   C. The Turtle

Think about it: What would you have done if you were Juan?

Draw it: Draw a picture of Juan and the turtle.

©2008 Plutarch Publications, Inc. PPI-1002   43

Name _____   Standard: Narrative Comprehension

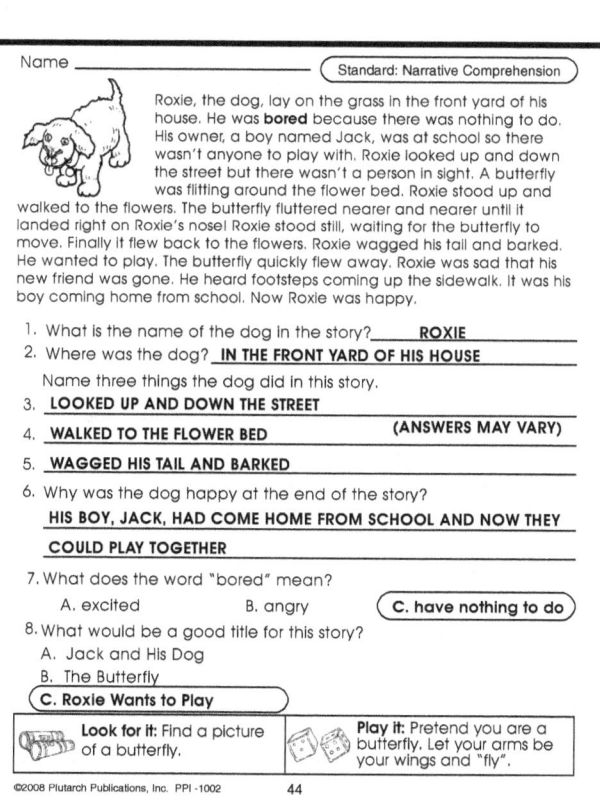

Roxie, the dog, lay on the grass in the front yard of his house. He was **bored** because there was nothing to do. His owner, a boy named Jack, was at school so there wasn't anyone to play with. Roxie looked up and down the street but there wasn't a person in sight. A butterfly was flitting around the flower bed. Roxie stood up and walked to the flowers. The butterfly fluttered nearer and nearer until it landed right on Roxie's nose! Roxie stood still, waiting for the butterfly to move. Finally it flew back to the flowers. Roxie wagged his tail and barked. He wanted to play. The butterfly quickly flew away. Roxie was sad that his new friend was gone. He heard footsteps coming up the sidewalk. It was his boy coming home from school. Now Roxie was happy.

1. What is the name of the dog in the story? __ROXIE__
2. Where was the dog? __IN THE FRONT YARD OF HIS HOUSE__

Name three things the dog did in this story.
3. __LOOKED UP AND DOWN THE STREET__
4. __WALKED TO THE FLOWER BED__   (ANSWERS MAY VARY)
5. __WAGGED HIS TAIL AND BARKED__
6. Why was the dog happy at the end of the story?
__HIS BOY, JACK, HAD COME HOME FROM SCHOOL AND NOW THEY__
__COULD PLAY TOGETHER__

7. What does the word "bored" mean?
   A. excited   B. angry   (**C. have nothing to do**)
8. What would be a good title for this story?
   A. Jack and His Dog
   B. The Butterfly
   (**C. Roxie Wants to Play**)

Look for it: Find a picture of a butterfly.

Play it: Pretend you are a butterfly. Let your arms be your wings and "fly".

©2008 Plutarch Publications, Inc. PPI-1002   44

Name _____   Standard: Narrative Comprehension

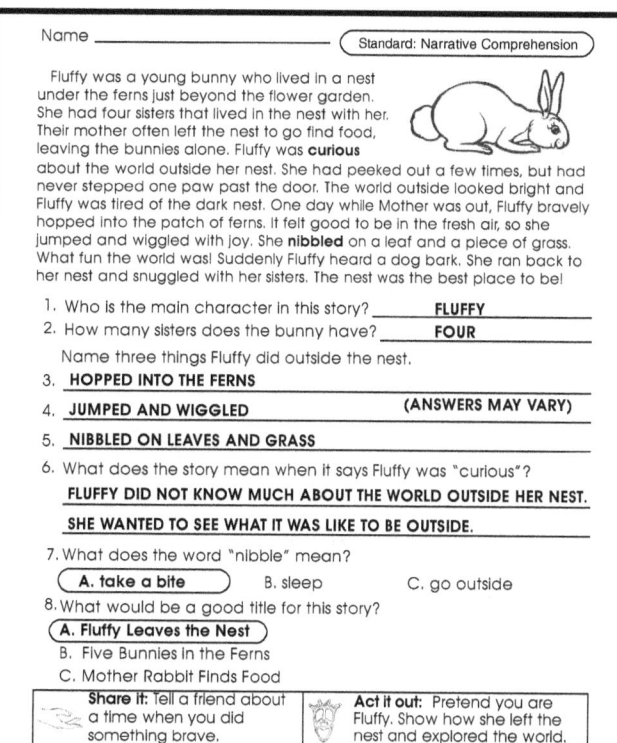

Fluffy was a young bunny who lived in a nest under the ferns just beyond the flower garden. She had four sisters that lived in the nest with her. Their mother often left the nest to go find food, leaving the bunnies alone. Fluffy was **curious** about the world outside her nest. She had peeked out a few times, but had never stepped one paw past the door. The world outside looked bright and Fluffy was tired of the dark nest. One day while Mother was out, Fluffy bravely hopped into the patch of ferns. It felt good to be in the fresh air, so she jumped and wiggled with joy. She **nibbled** on a leaf and a piece of grass. What fun this was! Suddenly Fluffy heard a dog bark. She ran back to her nest and snuggled with her sisters. The nest was the best place to be!

1. Who is the main character in this story? __FLUFFY__
2. How many sisters does the bunny have? __FOUR__

Name three things Fluffy did outside the nest.
3. __HOPPED INTO THE FERNS__
4. __JUMPED AND WIGGLED__   (ANSWERS MAY VARY)
5. __NIBBLED ON LEAVES AND GRASS__
6. What does the story mean when it says Fluffy was "curious"?
__FLUFFY DID NOT KNOW MUCH ABOUT THE WORLD OUTSIDE HER NEST.__
__SHE WANTED TO SEE WHAT IT WAS LIKE TO BE OUTSIDE.__

7. What does the word "nibble" mean?
   (**A. take a bite**)   B. sleep   C. go outside
8. What would be a good title for this story?
   (**A. Fluffy Leaves the Nest**)
   B. Five Bunnies in the Ferns
   C. Mother Rabbit Finds Food

Share it: Tell a friend about a time when you did something brave.

Act it out: Pretend you are Fluffy. Show how she left the nest and explored the world.

©2008 Plutarch Publications, Inc. PPI-1002   45

ANSWER KEYS: 46, 47, 48, 49

Name _____ *Standard: Narrative Comprehension*

James has a **hobby** that he really enjoys. He collects bugs! When James was four years old he got an Ant Farm for his birthday. He loved watching the ants as they dug tunnels and built nests. At five years old, James had three jars of dirt. One was for spiders, another for grasshoppers, and the last held beetles he had found under a log. For his sixth birthday, James got a little cage that could hold all kinds of bugs. He likes to catch the bugs, put them in the cage, and watch them for a few days. He thinks it is interesting to see what they eat and how they build their homes. He has learned many things about these **insects** and likes to share them with his class at school. Not everyone likes bugs, but James sure does!

1. Who is the main character in this story? **JAMES**
2. What does this boy like to do? **COLLECT BUGS**

Name three types of bugs that the boy has collected.
3. **ANTS**
4. **SPIDERS**
5. **GRASSHOPPERS/BEETLES**
6. What is a "hobby"?
   A HOBBY IS SOMETHING THAT YOU LIKE TO DO OFTEN
   (ANSWERS MAY VARY)
7. What is another word for "insect"?
   A. nest   **B. bug**   C. hobby
8. What would be a good title for this story?
   A. The Life of Insects
   B. James Has a Hobby
   C. Our Ant Farm

Look for it: See how many bugs you can find. Keep a list of their names.
Do it: Start a collection of something you like. Tell the class about it.

Name _____ *Standard: Narrative Comprehension*

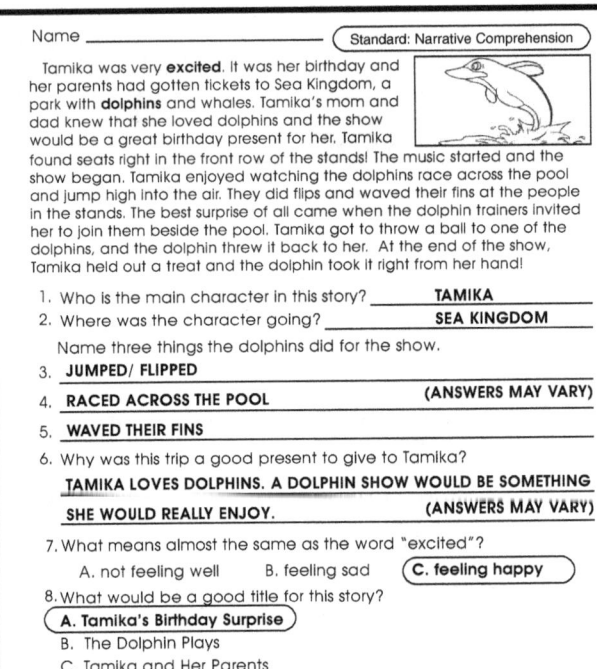

Tamika was very **excited**. It was her birthday and her parents had gotten tickets to Sea Kingdom, a park with **dolphins** and whales. Tamika's mom and dad knew that she loved dolphins and the show would be a great birthday present for her. Tamika found seats right in the front row of the stands! The music started and the show began. Tamika enjoyed watching the dolphins race across the pool and jump high into the air. They did flips and waved their fins at the people in the stands. The best surprise of all came when the dolphin trainers invited her to join them beside the pool. Tamika got to throw a ball to one of the dolphins, and the dolphin threw it back to her. At the end of the show, Tamika held out a treat and the dolphin took it right from her hand!

1. Who is the main character in this story? **TAMIKA**
2. Where was the character going? **SEA KINGDOM**

Name three things the dolphins did for the show.
3. **JUMPED/ FLIPPED**
4. **RACED ACROSS THE POOL**   (ANSWERS MAY VARY)
5. **WAVED THEIR FINS**
6. Why was this trip a good present to give to Tamika?
   TAMIKA LOVES DOLPHINS. A DOLPHIN SHOW WOULD BE SOMETHING SHE WOULD REALLY ENJOY.   (ANSWERS MAY VARY)
7. What means almost the same as the word "excited"?
   A. not feeling well   B. feeling sad   **C. feeling happy**
8. What would be a good title for this story?
   A. Tamika's Birthday Surprise
   B. The Dolphin Plays
   C. Tamika and Her Parents

Write about it: What would you like to do on your birthday?
Think about it: How are dolphins and whales alike?

Name _____ *Standard: Narrative Comprehension*

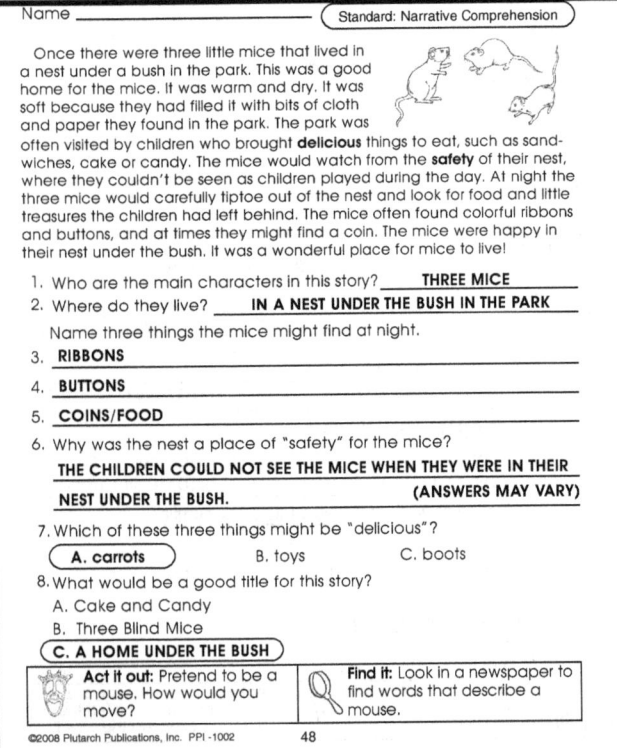

Once there were three little mice that lived in a nest under a bush in the park. This was a good home for the mice. It was warm and dry. It was soft because they had filled it with bits of cloth and paper they found in the park. The park was often visited by children who brought **delicious** things to eat, such as sandwiches, cake or candy. The mice would watch from the **safety** of their nest, where they couldn't be seen as children played during the day. At night the three mice carefully tiptoe out of the nest and look for food and little treasures the children had left behind. The mice often found colorful ribbons and buttons, and at times they might find a coin. The mice were happy in their nest under the bush. It was a wonderful place for mice to live!

1. Who are the main characters in this story? **THREE MICE**
2. Where do they live? **IN A NEST UNDER THE BUSH IN THE PARK**

Name three things the mice might find at night.
3. **RIBBONS**
4. **BUTTONS**
5. **COINS/FOOD**
6. Why was the nest a place of "safety" for the mice?
   THE CHILDREN COULD NOT SEE THE MICE WHEN THEY WERE IN THEIR NEST UNDER THE BUSH.   (ANSWERS MAY VARY)
7. Which of these three things might be "delicious"?
   A. carrots   B. toys   C. boots
8. What would be a good title for this story?
   A. Cake and Candy
   B. Three Blind Mice
   C. A HOME UNDER THE BUSH

Act it out: Pretend to be a mouse. How would you move?
Find it: Look in a newspaper to find words that describe a mouse.

Name _____ *Standard: Narrative Comprehension*

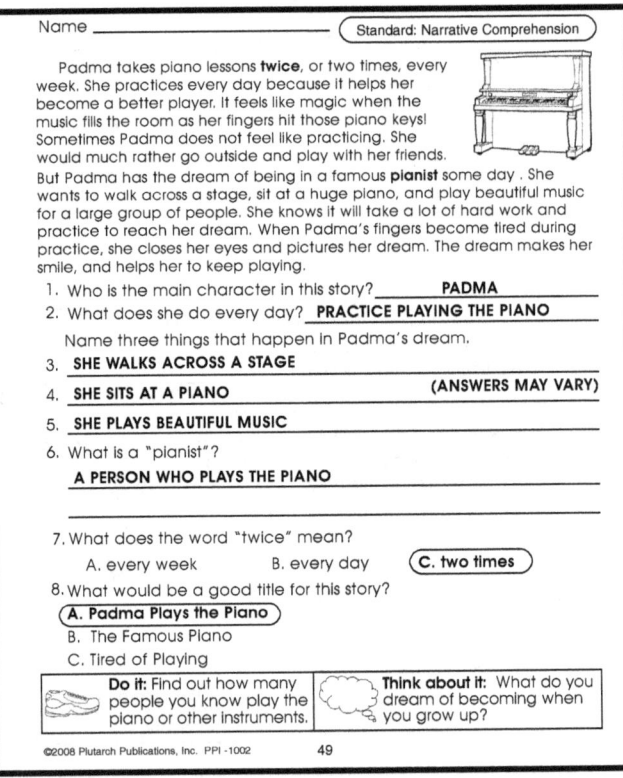

Padma takes piano lessons **twice**, or two times, every week. She practices every day because it helps her become a better player. It feels like magic when the music fills the room as her fingers hit those piano keys! Sometimes Padma does not feel like practicing. She would rather go outside and play with her friends. But Padma has the dream of being a famous **pianist** some day. She wants to walk across a stage, sit at a huge piano, and play beautiful music for a large group of people. She knows it will take a lot of hard work and practice to reach her dream. When Padma's fingers become tired during practice, she closes her eyes and pictures her dream. The dream makes her smile, and helps her to keep playing.

1. Who is the main character in this story? **PADMA**
2. What does she do every day? **PRACTICE PLAYING THE PIANO**

Name three things that happen in Padma's dream.
3. **SHE WALKS ACROSS A STAGE**
4. **SHE SITS AT A PIANO**   (ANSWERS MAY VARY)
5. **SHE PLAYS BEAUTIFUL MUSIC**
6. What is a "pianist"?
   A PERSON WHO PLAYS THE PIANO
7. What does the word "twice" mean?
   A. every week   B. every day   **C. two times**
8. What would be a good title for this story?
   A. Padma Plays the Piano
   B. The Famous Piano
   C. Tired of Playing

Do it: Find out how many people you know play the piano or other instruments.
Think about it: What do you dream of becoming when you grow up?

ANSWER KEYS: 50, 51, 52, 53

Name _____ Standard: Narrative Comprehension

Poor Peter was not feeling very happy. His father was taking him to the **dentist** today. The dentist was going to clean and x-ray his teeth to see if he had a **cavity**, or hole, that needed to be filled. Peter carefully brushed his teeth and then went to the dentist's office. He sat in a large chair. The dentist put a paper apron around Peter's neck and then took three x-ray pictures of his teeth. Peter opened his mouth wide so the dentist could clean his teeth. When he was finished cleaning, the dentist showed Peter the x-rays. There were no cavities and the dentist said his teeth looked healthy. The dentist gave Peter a new toothbrush and a tube of toothpaste. Peter was happy that his visit to the dentist was finally over!

1. Who is the main character in this story? __PETER__
2. Where was he going? __TO THE DENTIST__

   Name three things the dentist did.
3. __PUT A PAPER APRON AROUND PETER'S NECK__
4. __TOOK THREE X-RAYS OF PETER'S TEETH__   (ANSWERS MAY VARY)
5. __CLEANED PETER'S TEETH__
6. What is a "dentist"?
   __A PERSON WHO TAKES X-RAYS, CLEANS, AND TAKES CARE OF YOUR__
   __TEETH__   (ANSWERS MAY VARY)
7. What does the word "cavity" mean?
   A. clean teeth   **B. a hole**   C. to fill a tooth
8. What would be a good title for this story?
   A. Too Many Cavities
   B. Peter and His Father
   C. Peter Goes to the Dentist

Share it: Tell someone what happened on your last trip to the dentist.
Compare it: Do you feel like Peter when you go to the dentist?

©2008 Plutarch Publications, Inc. PPI-1002   50

Name _____ Standard: Narrative Comprehension

Maria went to the movie **theater** with her two best friends, Carla and Gina. They each bought a big bag of popcorn, a candy bar, and a cold drink. The girls found seats near the front of the theater where they could see everything. Maria sat between her friends and they talked until the lights **dimmed** and the room became almost dark. The movie started and the girls ate popcorn while they watched. It was a funny movie and the girls laughed a lot. Gina laughed so hard she had tears in her eyes. Maria laughed so hard she spilled her popcorn all over her lap! When the movie was over the girls agreed that was the funniest movie they had ever seen. Maria was glad she and her friends had so much fun.

1. Who is the main character in this story? __MARIA__
2. Who are her best friends? __CARLA AND GINA__

   Name three things the girls bought.
3. __A LARGE BAG OF POPCORN__
4. __A CANDY BAR__
5. __A COLD DRINK__
6. What happens when lights are "dimmed"?
   __THE ROOM BECOMES ALMOST DARK__
   (ANSWERS MAY VARY)
7. What is a "theater"?
   A. popcorn   B. a store   **C. a place for shows**
8. What would be a good title for this story?
   A. Maria and the Popcorn
   B. Fun at the Theater
   C. Carla and Gina are Friends

Find it: Look in the newspaper to see what movies are at your neighborhood theater.
Do it: Pop some popcorn and watch a funny movie with your friends.

©2008 Plutarch Publications, Inc. PPI-1002   51

Name _____ Standard: Expository Comprehension

Living or Nonliving?

Sorting things into **categories**, or groups, can help us better understand the world. Everything you see is LIVING or NONLIVING.

A person is living. A book is nonliving. Is a plant living? Yes, it is. There are seven characteristics (qualities) living things have but nonliving things do not. All living things can: 1) eat; 2) move; 3) grow; 4) **reproduce**, or have babies; 5) breathe; 6) remove waste; and 7) react to changes around them. It is easy to see how an animal is living, but a plant is harder to understand. Plants get food through their leaves and roots. They move by growing toward light. Plants are living things. Is jelly living or nonliving? Jelly is made from fruit. Fruit is part of a living plant, but jelly cannot eat or grow and it can't breathe or reproduce. Jelly is nonliving. All living things are either plants or animals.

Name the seven characteristics of living things.
1. __THEY CAN EAT__
2. __THEY CAN MOVE__
3. __THEY CAN GROW__
4. __THEY CAN REPRODUCE__   (ANSWERS MAY VARY)
5. __THEY CAN BREATHE__
6. __THEY CAN REMOVE WASTE__
7. __THEY CAN REACT TO CHANGES__
8. What is another word for "category"?
   A. living   **B. group**   C. person

Read the words. Write **L** if the item is living and **N** if it is nonliving.

__L__ 9. tree	__L__ 10. horse	__N__ 11. bread
__N__ 12. log	__L__ 13. grass	__N__ 14. ball
__N__ 15. lamp	__N__ 16. rain	__N__ 17. boat
__L__ 18. butterfly	__L__ 19. ant	__L__ 20. fish

Look for it: Look around your room. Make a list of six things that you can see. Tell if each one is living or nonliving.

©2008 Plutarch Publications, Inc. PPI-1002   52

Name _____ Standard: Expository Comprehension

Plants

Plants, although they do not move much, are living things. They eat food that they make from sunshine and water taken in through their roots and leaves. Plants **respire**, or "breathe" by taking in gases from the air. They **expel**, or get rid of, gases they don't use. When they get enough water and sunshine, plants will react by growing. When they don't get enough, they react by losing leaves, turning brown in spots, or dying. Most plants reproduce by making seeds. Some seeds are **produced** (made) in the flower of plants such trees, vegetables, and grass. Plants such as pine trees and tulips produce seeds in a cone or bulb. Ferns and some seaweeds produce spores, another type of seed. Plants are important to people and other animals. Much of the food we eat comes from plants. Also, a lot of the medicines we take comes from plants.

1. What is the title of this story? __PLANTS__
2. What does the word "respire" mean? __BREATHE__

   Name three things that prove a plant is a living thing.
3. __THEY MOVE / THEY RESPIRE__
4. __THEY REACT/THEY REPRODUCE__   (ANSWERS MAY VARY)
5. __THEY GROW__
6. What is another word for "produce"?
   A. make   B. die   C. grow
7. How do most plants reproduce? __THEY MAKE SEEDS__
8. What does the word "expel" mean? __TO GET RID OF__

Read the words. Write **P** if the food comes from a plant and **A** if it comes from an animal.

__P__ 9. beans	__P__ 10. corn	__A__ 11. milk
__P__ 12. bread	__A__ 13. egg	__P__ 14. peas
__P__ 15. carrot	__A__ 16. ham	__P__ 17. potato
__A__ 18. cheese	__A__ 19. meat	__P__ 20. rice

Find it: Look in the newspaper for grocery store ads. Make a list of the foods advertised. Decide if they are foods from plants or animals.

©2008 Plutarch Publications, Inc. PPI-1002   53

©2008 Plutarch Publications, Inc. PPI-1002

ANSWER KEYS: 54, 55, 56, 57

Page 54

Name _____ *Standard: Expository Comprehension*

Animals

Animals are living things. Just like plants, they eat, grow, breathe, and reproduce. However, animals can move about easily while plants hardly move at all. Animals can walk, fly, crawl, run, hop, skip, trot, and roll. Animals react with the world around them by using their **senses** of sight, hearing, smell, taste, and touch. Animals come in all shapes and sizes. Dinosaurs and **humans** (people) are animals, and so are bugs and worms. There are even some animals that are too tiny to see without a microscope! With so many types of animals, it was difficult to understand much about them. **Aristotle**, a man who lived over two thousand years ago, helped solve this problem by sorting all animals into categories. He grouped them by the things they had **in common**, or shared.

1. What is this story about? **ANIMALS**
2. What do animals do easily that plants can hardly do? **MOVE**

   Name three of the five senses listed in the story.
3. **SIGHT** OR **TASTE**
4. **HEARING** OR **TOUCH**   (ANSWERS MAY VARY)
5. **SMELL**
6. What is another word for "human"?
   A. animal   B. sense   **(C. person)**
7. What does a microscope do? **HELP YOU SEE TINY THINGS**
8. What does the phrase "in common" mean? **SHARED**

Which sense would be used for each item below? On the blank, write **S** for SIGHT or **H** for HEARING.

- **S** 9. a butterfly
- **H** 10. singing
- **H** 11. music
- **H** 12. a car horn
- **S** 13. reading
- **H** 14. snoring
- **H** 15. a voice
- **S** 16. a picture
- **S** 17. goldfish
- **S** 18. clouds
- **H** 19. a doorbell
- **S** 20. a plant

Make it: Start a scrapbook of animals. Find pictures of the animals you like and paste them in your book. Label them.

Page 55

Name _____ *Standard: Expository Comprehension*

Mammals

It is easier to understand animals if they are sorted into groups or **classes**. The class that has the most animals is called mammals. Mammals can be as small as two inches, like the shrew which is a type of mole. They can also be as large as 100 feet long, like the blue whale. Some mammals walk on two legs, others walk on four legs, some have no legs, and some even fly! What makes mammals different from other animals? They have several common characteristics that all mammals share: 1) Mammals have a **spine**, or backbone; 2) Their bodies are covered with fur or hair; 3) They produce milk to feed their young; 4) Mammals give birth to live babies; and 5) Mammals are **warm-blooded** which means they make their own body heat. Humans are in this class of animals called mammals.

Name the five characteristics of mammals.
1. **THEY HAVE A SPINE OR BACKBONE**
2. **THEY HAVE HAIR OR FUR**
3. **THEY PRODUCE MILK**
4. **THEY GIVE BIRTH TO LIVE BABIES**   (ANSWERS MAY VARY)
5. **THEY ARE WARM-BLOODED**
6. Which word means the animal can make its own heat?
   A. mammal   B. spine   **(C. warm-blooded)**
7. What is another word for "group"? **CLASS**
8. What is another word for "backbone"? **SPINE**

Use the five characteristics of a mammal to decide if the animals below are mammals. Write **M** if it is a mammal and **N** if it is not.

- **N** 9. frog
- **M** 10. goat
- **N** 11. fish
- **M** 12. dog
- **N** 13. snake
- **M** 14. rabbit
- **M** 15. deer
- **N** 16. spider
- **M** 17. cat
- **M** 18. raccoon
- **N** 19. ant
- **N** 20. bee

Do it: Time yourself and a friend. See how many mammals each of you can list in ten minutes. Compare your lists. How many mammals did you list in all?

Page 56

Name _____ *Standard: Expository Comprehension*

Birds

The class of animals known as birds can be found anywhere on Earth, from jungles to the ice caps at the north pole. Birds are not difficult to tell apart from most other animals. They have two characteristics that are the same as mammals: 1) All birds have a spine; and 2) They are warm-blooded. Birds have five other characteristics that make them very different from other animals: 3) Birds are covered with feathers; 4) They have a bill, or beak, but no teeth; 5) Not all birds can fly, but all of them do have wings; 6) Birds lay eggs and keep them warm until the babies are big enough to **hatch**, or break out on their own; and 7) Birds have a **wishbone** in their chest. This wishbone bends in to allow the bird to flap its wings. It also pushes out to keep the wings from crushing the chest.

Name the seven characteristics of birds.
1. **THEY HAVE A SPINE**
2. **THEY ARE WARM-BLOODED**
3. **THEY HAVE FEATHERS**   (ANSWERS MAY VARY)
4. **THEY HAVE A BILL OR BEAK WITH NO TEETH**
5. **THEY HAVE WINGS**
6. **THEY LAY EGGS**
7. **THEY HAVE A WISHBONE**
8. Which word means "to come out of an egg"?
   (A. hatch)   B. wishbone   C. jungle

Write **B** if the word is a characteristic of birds. Write **N** if it is not.

- **B** 9. wings
- **N** 10. live birth
- **B** 11. spine
- **N** 12. fins
- **B** 13. feathers
- **N** 14. hair
- **N** 15. teeth
- **B** 16. wishbone
- **N** 17. fur
- **B** 18. warm blooded
- **B** 19. beak
- **B** 20. eggs

Look for it: Go for a walk or look out your window and keep a count of how many birds you see. Find a book on birds and find what kind they are. Any crows? Robins? Herons?

Page 57

Name _____ *Standard: Expository Comprehension*

Fish

Fish are a class of animals that live in water all around the world. They can be found in ponds, rivers, lakes, oceans, fresh water, and salt water. Fish have seven characteristics, two of which are like mammals or birds: 1) Fish have spines like mammals and birds; 2) Most fish lay eggs, just like birds, but some fish do give birth to live babies, just like mammals; 3) Their bodies are covered with scales; 4) Fish live their whole lives in water; 5) They have **fins** instead of arms or legs; 6) Fish have gills, a special body part, that takes the air from the water so they can breathe; and 7) Fish cannot make their own heat, so they are cold-blooded. They get heat from the water where they live or by sitting where the sun shines on them. As the water warms or cools, the fish get warmer or colder as well.

Name the seven characteristics of fish.
1. **THEY HAVE SPINES**
2. **MOST LAY EGGS BUT SOME HAVE LIVE BIRTH**
3. **THEY ARE COVERED WITH SCALES**   (ANSWERS MAY VARY)
4. **THEY LIVE IN WATER**
5. **THEY HAVE FINS**
6. **THEY HAVE GILLS**
7. **THEY ARE COLD-BLOODED**
8. What do fish have instead of arms or legs? **FINS**

Read the words below. Write **F** if the word is a characteristic of fish. Write **N** if it is not.

- **N** 9. warm-blooded
- **N** 10. beak
- **F** 11. fins
- **F** 12. scales
- **N** 13. hair
- **F** 14. spine
- **F** 15. live in water
- **N** 16. feathers
- **F** 17. lay eggs
- **N** 18. live on land
- **F** 19. cold-blooded
- **F** 20. gills

Compare it: Think about how different animals move. Make a list of animals that swim, fly, walk, and slide. Some animals may move in more than one way!

ANSWER KEYS: 58, 59, 60, 61

Name _____ *Standard: Expository Comprehension*

Reptiles

Reptiles are a class of animals that usually live on land, but often are very close to the water. This class includes snakes, turtles, lizards, crocodiles, alligators and other animals that are now **extinct** (died out) like the dinosaurs. Reptiles have some of the same characteristics of mammals and fish but a few things make them different: 1) Reptiles have a spine; 2) Like fish, they are cold-blooded; 3) Reptiles lay eggs in nests on land, like birds, but they do not take care of the young; 4) The skin of reptiles is dry and covered with small scales; 5) Reptiles have claws on their toes unless they do not have legs, like a snake or lizard without legs; and 6) Although reptiles may spend a lot of time in water they have lungs for breathing, just like mammals.

Name the six characteristics of reptiles.
1. THEY HAVE A SPINE
2. THEY ARE COLD-BLOODED
3. THEY LAY EGGS
4. THEIR SKIN IS DRY AND HAS SCALES
5. THEY HAVE CLAWS IF THEY HAVE TOES
6. THEY HAVE LUNGS

Name two characteristics that birds and reptiles share:
7. THEY BOTH LAY EGGS/ THEY HAVE LUNGS
8. THEY HAVE SPINES/THEY HAVE CLAWS (ANSWERS MAY VARY)

Read the words. Write **R** if the animal is a reptile and **N** if it is not.
- **R** 9. box turtle
- **R** 10. rattle snake
- **R** 11. gecko
- **N** 12. goldfish
- **N** 13. beaver
- **N** 14. mouse
- **R** 15. Komodo dragon
- **R** 16. tortoise
- **N** 17. fly
- **N** 18. snail
- **R** 19. alligator
- **N** 20. bat

Think about it: Dinosaurs were reptiles. Which reptile that exists today is most like the dinosaur? Which characteristics do they share?

Name _____ *Standard: Expository Comprehension*

Amphibians

The word amphibian means "double life". Most amphibians spend half of their lives in water and the other half on land. Frogs, toads, newts and salamanders are all amphibians. Characteristics of amphibians are: 1) They have spines; 2) They are cold-blooded; 3) They are hatched from eggs; 4) They have lungs, but they also breathe through their skin; 5) The skin of reptiles is smooth without hair, fur, feathers, or scales; 6) Reptiles must keep their skin wet, so they live in wet places; and 7) Although most have toes, they do not have claws. Many amphibians go through a change called **metamorphosis**. Frogs are born as fish-like tadpoles, breathing with gills. As they grow, they develop legs and lungs then lose the gills and tail. They spend their adult lives living on land.

Name the seven characteristics of amphibians.
1. THEY HAVE SPINES
2. THEY ARE COLD-BLOODED
3. THEY HATCH FROM EGGS
4. THEY HAVE LUNGS   (ANSWERS MAY VARY)
5. THEY HAVE SMOOTH SKIN
6. THEY LIVE IN WET PLACES
7. THEY DO NOT HAVE CLAWS

8. What word means "a change from one thing to another"?
   A. metamorphosis   B. amphibian   C. tadpole

Write **A** if the word is a characteristic of amphibians. Write **N** if it is not.
- **A** 9. cold-blooded
- **N** 10. scales
- **A** 11. eggs
- **A** 12. smooth skin
- **A** 13. no claws
- **N** 14. claws
- **A** 15. live near water
- **N** 16. can fly
- **A** 17. lungs
- **N** 18. dry skin
- **A** 19. has a spine
- **N** 20. hair

Find it: Look online or in an encyclopedia to find the life cycle of a frog. Draw a chart and explain it to a friend or adult.

Name _____ *Standard: Expository Comprehension*

Insects

There are more insects on earth than any other class of animal. In fact, 95% of all animals are insects! They can live almost anywhere on Earth, including the ice caps at the north pole, but not many are found in the ocean. There are five main characteristics of insects: 1) Insects have three parts to their bodies including the head, thorax (chest) and abdomen (stomach); 2) They have six legs; 3) All insects have two pairs of wings and can fly; 4) Insects go through a metamorphosis and have four life stages. First they are eggs, then larva (like a worm), then they become a pupa (cocoon) and finally they are adults; and 5) Most adult insects have antennae or "feelers" on their head. They use the antennae to help them see, feel, smell and taste the world around them.

Name four of the five characteristics of insects.
1. THEY HAVE A HEAD, THORAX, AND ABDOMEN
2. THEY HAVE SIX LEGS/ THEY HAVE ANTENNAE
3. THEY HAVE TWO PAIRS OF WINGS
4. THEY HAVE FOUR LIFE STAGES   (ANSWERS MAY VARY)

Name four life stages in the metamorphosis of an insect.
5. THE EGG IS LAID AND HATCHES
6. THE INSECT IS A LARVA. IT LOOKS LIKE A WORM.
7. THE LARVA MAKES A PUPA, OR A COCOON, TO PROTECT ITSELF
8. THE ADULT COMES OUT OF THE PUPA

Read the animal names. Write **S** if it is an insect and **N** if it is not.
- **N** 9. robin
- **S** 10. butterfly
- **N** 11. squirrel
- **S** 12. grasshopper
- **N** 13. worm
- **S** 14. fly
- **S** 15. cricket
- **S** 16. beetle
- **N** 17. duck
- **N** 18. bat
- **S** 19. mosquito
- **N** 20. spider

Draw it: Find an insect and draw a picture of it. Label the head, thorax, and abdomen. Does it have antennae?

Name _____ *Standard: Functional Comprehension*

1. What is the name of this poem?
   THE LEAF

2. In the first group of sentences, which season is coming?
   WINTER

3. In the first group of sentences, which word rhymes with "way"?
   STAY

4. In the second group of sentences, what color did the leaf turn?
   RED

5. In the second group of sentences, which word rhymes with "go"?
   SNOW

6. In the third group of sentences, which season is coming?
   SPRING

7. In the third group of sentences, what was singing?
   BIRDS

The Leaf

The cold winds blew.
Winter was on the way.
Most of the trees were bare,
But one leaf chose to stay.

It turned from green to red,
Got covered up with snow,
Stayed through the icy days.
But it wouldn't let go.

When days began to warm,
And birds began to sing,
The leaf was glad because
it had lasted until the spring!

List the three changes in the weather the poem describes.
8. **AT FIRST IT WAS WINDY,**
9. **THEN IT WAS COLD AND SNOWY**   (ANSWERS MAY VARY)
10. **AND FINALLY IT WARMED UP**

11. At the end of the poem, why was the leaf happy?
    IT HAD MADE IT THROUGH THE WINTER TO SEE SPRING

Say it: Read the poem quietly to yourself. Now read it aloud to a friend or teacher.

ANSWER KEYS: 62, 63, 64, 65

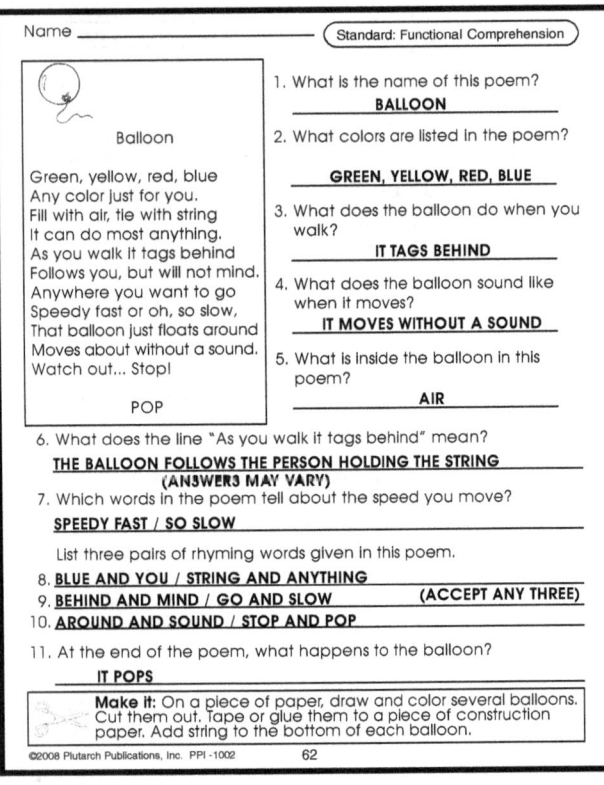

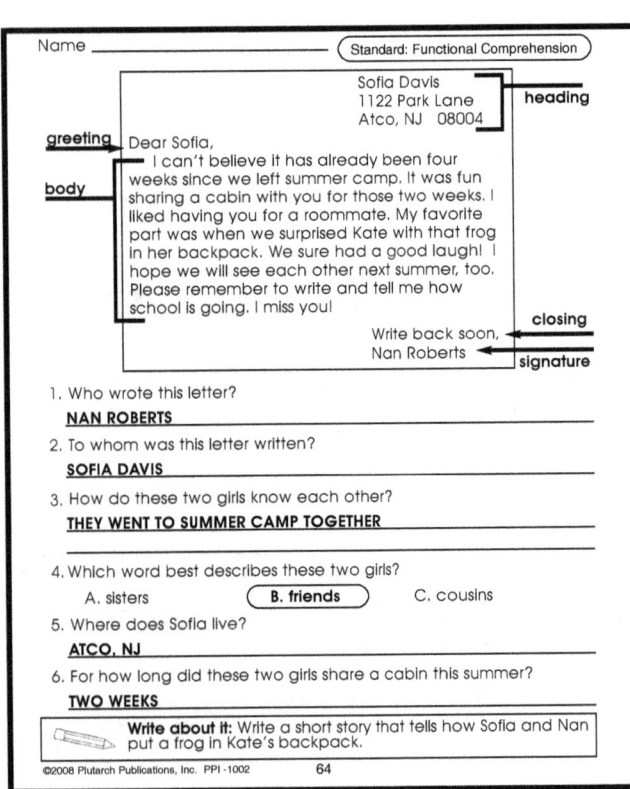

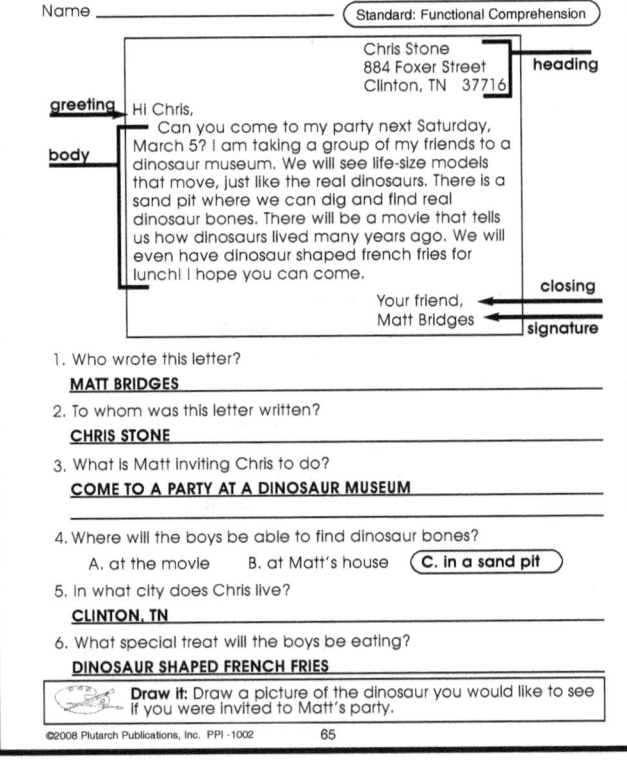

ANSWER KEYS: 66, 67, 68, 69

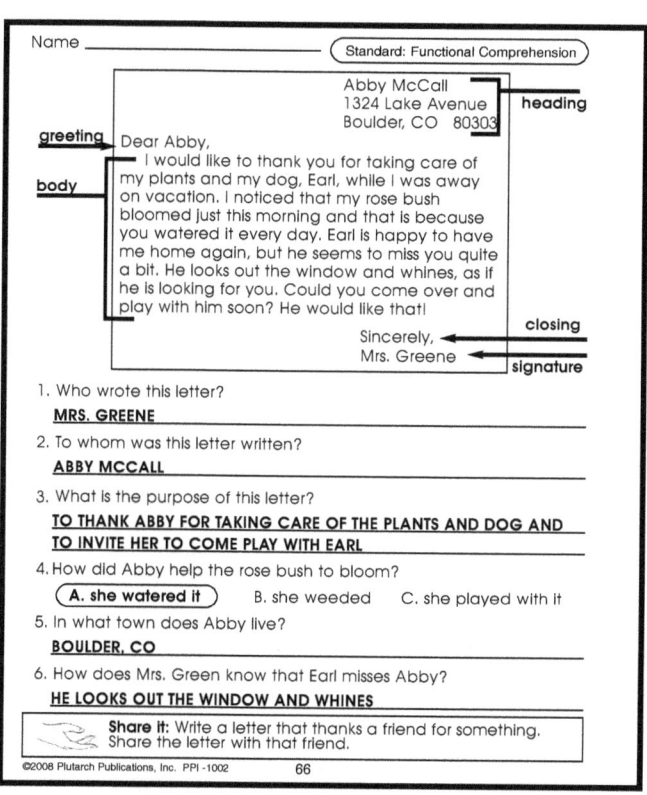

1. Who wrote this letter?
   MRS. GREENE
2. To whom was this letter written?
   ABBY MCCALL
3. What is the purpose of this letter?
   TO THANK ABBY FOR TAKING CARE OF THE PLANTS AND DOG AND TO INVITE HER TO COME PLAY WITH EARL
4. How did Abby help the rose bush to bloom?
   A. she watered it   B. she weeded   C. she played with it
5. In what town does Abby live?
   BOULDER, CO
6. How does Mrs. Green know that Earl misses Abby?
   HE LOOKS OUT THE WINDOW AND WHINES

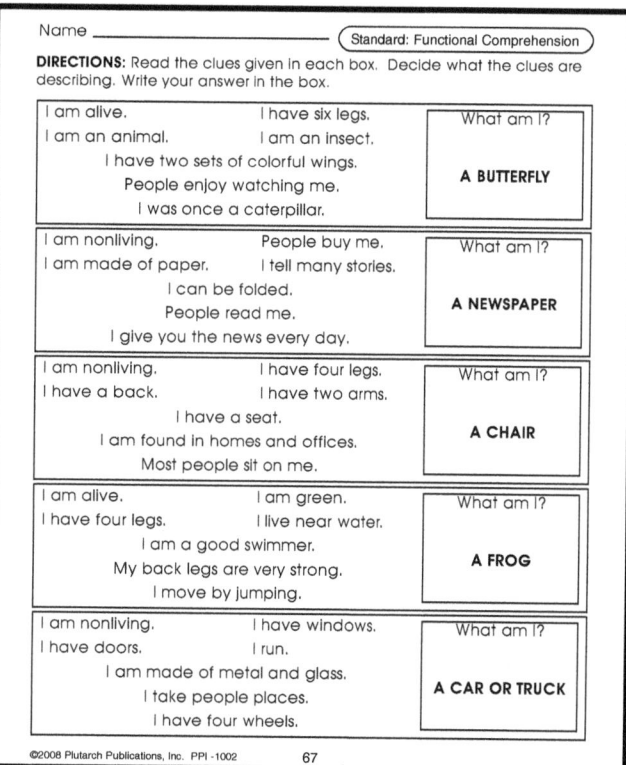

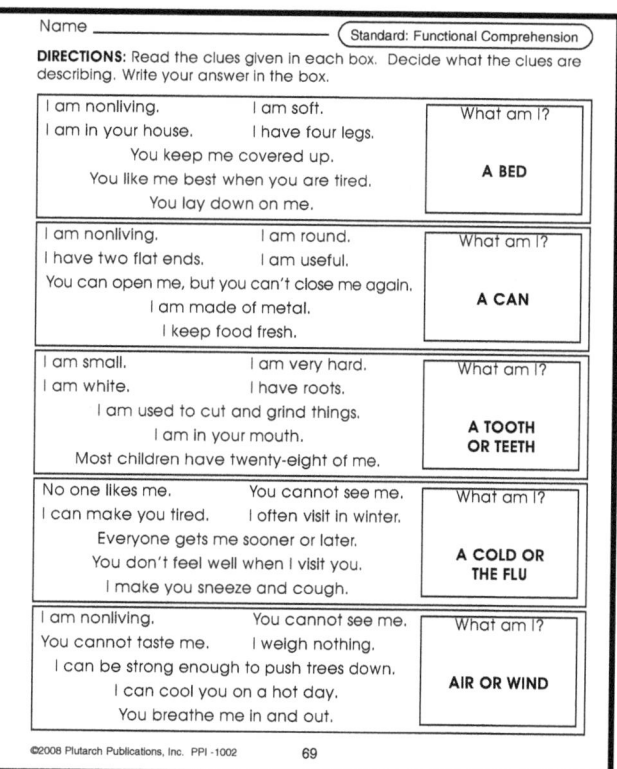

www.ingramcontent.com/pod-product-compliance
Lightning Source LLC
Chambersburg PA
CBHW081018040426
42444CB00014B/3255